Easy to Use

PICK UP & PLAY

CHORD
PROGRESSIONS

LEARN & WRITE 100S OF SONGS

SEE IT ▪ HEAR IT

JAKE JACKSON

T0303423

Flame Tree Music

mobile
online
in print

Flame Tree Music
BOOKS ▪ eBOOKS ▪ RESOURCES

Contents

Publisher/Creative Director: Nick Wells • Project Editor: Gillian Whitaker
Website and Software: David Neville with Stevens Dumpala and Steve Moulton

First published 2018 by
FLAME TREE PUBLISHING
6 Melbray Mews, Fulham,
London SW6 3NS, United Kingdom
flametreepublishing.com

Music information site: flametreemusic.com

23 • 3 4 5 6 7 8 9 10

© 2018 Flame Tree Publishing Ltd

The CIP record for this book is available from the British Library.

ISBN: 978-1-78664-780-1

All images and notation courtesy of Flame Tree Publishing Ltd, except the following guitar diagrams © 2018 Jake Jackson/Flame Tree Publishing LTs. Courtesy of Shutterstock.com and © the following contributors: BlueSkyImage 9; Africa Studio 21; Antonio Guillem 27; DEALORY 30; Pepsco Studio 33b, 33l, 33r, 33t; Tiffany Bryant 37; Anzhelika Voloshyna 51; Stokkete 57, 153; Wally Stemberger 71; Emotions studio 77; Andrii Muzyka 91; Rawpixel.com 97, 149, 160; Brian A Jackson 111; Alexander Raths 117; Viachaslau Kraskouski 133; Shanti Hesse 146; Sasa Prudkov 166; Dmitry A 167; Magdalena Wielobob 171.

Every effort has been made to contact copyright holders. We apologize in advance for any omissions and would be pleased to insert the appropriate acknowledgement in subsequent editions of this publication.

Android is a trademark of Google Inc. Logic Pro, iPhone and iPad are either registered trademarks or trademarks of Apple Computer Inc. in the United States and/or other countries. Cubase is a registered trademark or trademark of Steinberg Media Technologies GmbH, a wholly owned subsidiary of Yamaha Corporation, in the United States and/or other countries. Nokia's product names are either trademarks or registered trademarks of Nokia. Nokia is a registered trademark of Nokia Corporation in the United States and/or other countries. Samsung and Galaxy S are both registered trademarks of Samsung Electronics America, Ltd. in the United States and/or other countries.

Jake Jackson (author) is a writer and musician. He has created and contributed to over 30 practical music books, including *Guitar Chords* and *How to Play Guitar*. His music is available on iTunes, Amazon and Spotify amongst others.

Thanks to **Alan Brown** (for some of the musical examples)

Printed in China

Chord Progressions
An Introduction

Many songs consist of a short chord sequence that is repeated throughout. With just a few chords, it is possible to learn hundreds of songs, play along with others, and experiment with creating your own songs. In this book you'll find:

1. The most popular chord progressions, with chord names and diagrams clearly laid out for the most common keys.

2. Structures for the main chord progressions and their variations that can be easily applied to any key, as well as examples of the progressions in action.

3. General advice on recognizing patterns, with concise information on chords and how they relate to keys and scales.

4. Sections on further techniques and composition, which encourage experimentation and offer tips on creating and embellishing your own chord patterns.

5. QR code links to **flametreemusic.com**, an extensive audio library of chords and scales.

When playing chord progressions, the clearer your knowledge of the chords involved and how they relate to one another, the easier it will be to adapt to new keys, new structures, and new musical ideas. This book aims to put chord progressions in context, to provide you with a framework to write your own songs as well as follow given structures in existing music.

The Diagrams
A Quick Guide

START
HERE

THE
BASICS

I V vi IV

I IV V

ii V I

I vi IV V

BEYOND
BASICS

WRITING
SONGS

The majority of diagrams in this book are for chord shapes, though there will also be some examples of progressions and scales in standard and TAB notation. While some musical knowledge is assumed, the below is provided as a reference.

Standard Notation

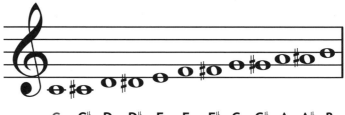

C   C♯   D   D♯   E   F   F♯   G   G♯   A   A♯   B

TAB Notation

Some guitarists prefer to use tablature (called TAB) instead of staves. The six lines represent the six strings of the guitar, from the high E string to the low E string, and the numbers represent the frets that produce the notes. A zero indicates that the string is played open. In the below example, the first C is played on the 5th string – the A string – by holding down the third fret along.

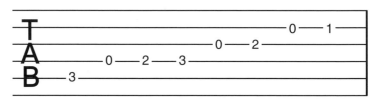

C   D   E   F   G   A   B   C

FREE ACCESS on iPhone & Android
etc, using any free QR code app

Scan to **HEAR** the C major chord, and access the full library of scales and chords on flametreemusic.com

Chord Diagrams

The Strings: The bass E appears on the left (6th string).
The top E is on the right (1st string).
The top E is the E above **middle C** on the piano.

Fingerings:

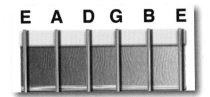

1 is the index finger   **2** is the middle finger
3 is the ring finger   **4** is the little finger

String isn't played
Open string position
Nut at the top of the neck

X   O

The 1st fret*

Finger position for the notes

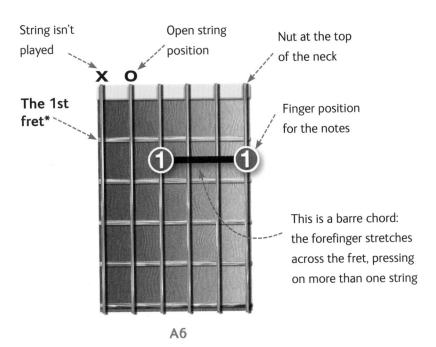

This is a barre chord: the forefinger stretches across the fret, pressing on more than one string

A6

* When the chord position isn't as close to the nut, a number to the left indicates the changed location on the fretboard. E.g. a '2' means the diagram starts from the 2nd fret rather than the 1st.

THE BASICS

I V vi IV

I IV V

ii V I

I vi IV V

BEYOND BASICS

WRITING SONGS

START HERE

START
HERE

The Sound Links
Another Quick Guide

THE
BASICS

I V vi IV

I IV V

ii V I

Requirements: a camera and internet-ready smartphone (e.g. **iPhone**, any **Android** phone (e.g. **Samsung Galaxy**), **Nokia Lumia**, or **camera-enabled tablet** such as the **iPad Mini**). The best result is achieved using a WIFI connection.

1. Download any **free QR code reader**. An app store search will reveal a great many of these, so obviously it's best to go with the ones with the highest ratings and don't be afraid to try a few before you settle on the one that works best for you. Tapmedia's QR Reader app is good, or ATT Scanner (used below) or QR Media. Some of the free apps have ads, which can be annoying.

2. On your smartphone, open the app and **scan** the **QR code** at the base of any particular page.

FREE ACCESS on iPhone & Android etc, using any free QR code app

Scan to HEAR the C major chord, and access the full library of scales and chords on flametreemusic.com

6

I vi IV V

3. Scanning the chord will bring you to the C major chord, and from there you can access and hear the complete library of scales and chords on flametreemusic.com.

BEYOND
BASICS

WRITING
SONGS

FREE ACCESS on iPhone & Android etc, using any free QR code app

Scan to **HEAR** the C major chord, and access the full library of scales and chords on flametreemusic.com

On pages where QR codes feature alongside particular chords and scales, those codes will directly take you to the relevant chord or scale on the website.

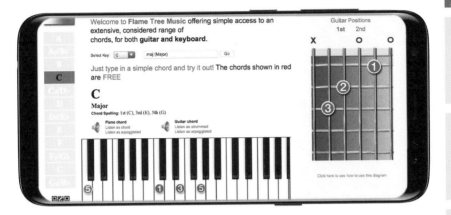

4. Use the drop down menu to choose from **20 scales** or 12 **free chords** (50 with subscription) per key.

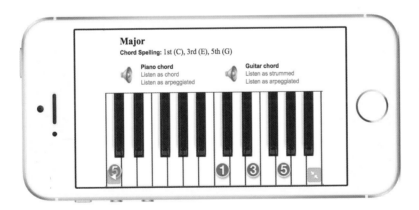

5. Click the sounds! Both piano and guitar audio is provided. This is particularly helpful when you're playing with others.

The QR codes give you direct access to chords and scales You can access a much wider range of chords if you register and subscribe.

FREE ACCESS on iPhone & Android etc, using any free QR code app

Scan to **HEAR** the C major chord, and access the full library of scales and chords on flametreemusic.com

START HERE

THE BASICS

I V vi IV

I IV V

ii V I

I vi IV V

BEYOND BASICS

WRITING SONGS

START
HERE

THE
BASICS

I V vi IV

I IV V

ii V I

I vi IV V

BEYOND
BASICS

WRITING
SONGS

What Is a Chord Progression?

A chord progression is a series of chords that is often repeated throughout a song. Chord progressions support the melody and provide the framework for the overall musical structure.

Some chord combinations are more popular than others, due to the way they sound together. Understanding the relationship between chords and the notes within them will enable you to recognize typical patterns and create your own versions too. This chapter introduces the basic concepts behind chord construction and how this leads to particular chords being favoured over others in chord progressions.

This section will cover:

- **Chord symbols, the fretboard and rhythm-guitar playing**
- **The relationship between chords, keys and scales**
- **Using major scales to build chord progressions**
- **Transposing chord progressions to other keys**
- **The most common chords in the most common keys**
- **Basic techniques for playing chords on the guitar**
- **Tips for smooth chord transitions**
- **Common types of chord progression**

FREE ACCESS on iPhone & Android etc, using any free QR code app

Scan to **HEAR** the C major chord, and access the full library of scales and chords on flametreemusic.com

START HERE

THE BASICS

I V vi IV

I IV V

ii V I

I vi IV V

BEYOND BASICS

WRITING SONGS

FREE ACCESS on iPhone & Android etc, using any free QR code app

Scan to **HEAR** the C major chord, and access the full library of scales and chords on flametreemusic.com

9

Chord Symbols

START HERE

THE BASICS

I V vi IV

I IV V

ii V I

I vi IV V

BEYOND BASICS

WRITING SONGS

There are two main types of chords that form the core of most popular music: major chords and minor chords.

Major Chords

The chord symbol that tells you when to play a major chord is simply the letter name of the chord written as a capital. For example, the chord symbol for the G major chord is 'G'; and the chord symbol for the D major chord is 'D'. Major chords have a bright, strong sound.

Minor Chords

Minor chord symbols consist of the capital letter of the chord name followed by a lowercase 'm'. For example, the chord symbol for the E minor chord is 'Em' and chord symbol for the A minor chord is 'Am'. Minor chords have a mellow, sombre sound.

Other Chords

Although there are dozens of different chord types that exist in music, all of them stem from the basic major and minor triads. Other chord types tend to just extend or vary the notes of the major or minor triads using other notes from the key.

Opposite, the most common chord types and their symbols are shown for the key of C. Not all of these chord types are present in this book, but being able to recognize the symbols will be useful, as they tell you which notes from the key are needed to form the chord.

FREE ACCESS on iPhone & Android etc, using any free QR code app

Scan to **HEAR** the C major chord, and access the full library of scales and chords on flametreemusic.com

Chord Name	Chord Symbol	Chord Notes
C major	**C**	C, E, G
C minor	**Cm**	C, E♭, G
C augmented triad	**C+**	C, E, G♯
C diminished triad	**C°**	C, E♭, G♭
C suspended 2nd	**Csus2**	C, D, G
C suspended 4th	**Csus4**	C, F, G
C 5th (power) chord	**C5**	C, G
C major 6th	**C6**	C, E, G, A
C minor 6th	**Cm6**	C, E♭, G, A
C dominant 7th	**C7**	C, E, G, B♭
C major 7th	**Cmaj7**	C, E, G, B
C minor 7th	**Cm7**	C, E♭, G, B♭
C half diminished 7th	**Cø7 or Cm7♭5**	C, E♭, G♭, B♭
C diminished 7th	**C°7**	C, E♭, G♭, B♭♭
C minor major 7th	**Cm(maj7)**	C, E♭, G, B
C dominant 7th ♯5	**C7+5**	C, E, G♯, B♭
C dominant 7th ♭5	**C7♭5**	C, E, G♭, B♭
C major add 9	**Cadd9**	C, E, G, D
C dominant 9th	**C9**	C, E, G, B♭, D
C major 9th	**Cmaj9**	C, E, G, B, D
C minor 9th	**Cm9**	C, E♭, G, B♭
C dominant 11th	**C11**	C, E, G, B♭, D, F
C dominant 13th	**C13**	C, E, G, B♭, D, A

START HERE

THE BASICS

I V vi IV

I IV V

ii V I

I vi IV V

BEYOND BASICS

WRITING SONGS

FREE ACCESS on iPhone & Android etc, using any free QR code app

Scan to **HEAR** the C major chord, and access the full library of scales and chords on flametreemusic.com

General Tips

It's always useful to have a clear idea of where each note lies in relation to other notes. On the guitar, the frets are organized in semitone intervals.

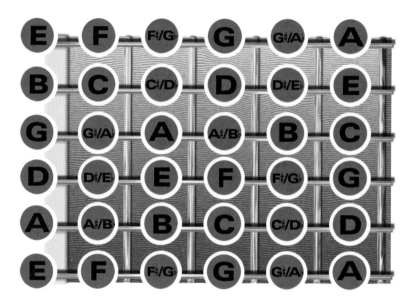

Guitar fingerboard with nut on the left, bass strings at the bottom, high E string at the top

Because the guitar has a three to four octave range, and some notes can be played at exactly the same pitch in several **fingerboard positions**, the harmonic possibilities on the instrument are almost endless: even simple major or minor chords can be played in numerous fingerboard positions – each with a multitude of possible fingerings.

Use shapes that suit your fingers and that work well with the other chord shapes you're playing in the song. Often you'll find that, rather than having to jump around the fingerboard to play the next chord in a song, you can devise an **alternative fingering** near to the previous chord.

FREE ACCESS on iPhone & Android etc, using any free QR code app

Scan to **HEAR** the C major chord, and access the full library of scales and chords on flametreemusic.com

START
HERE

THE
BASICS

I V vi IV

I IV V

ii V I

I vi IV V

BEYOND
BASICS

WRITING
SONGS

Rhythm Guitar

START HERE

THE BASICS

I V vi IV

I IV V

ii V I

I vi IV V

BEYOND BASICS

WRITING SONGS

While featuring in other guitar parts, chord progressions are a major feature of rhythm-guitar playing, as they provide the backbone for the song both musically and rhythmically.

Some useful skills to develop for both rhythm-guitar playing and chord progressions generally include:

- **Timing: practicing with a metronome, timer app, drum machine or backing tracks**
- **Fluent changes between chords: see pages 28-33 for tips on smooth transition techniques**
- **A clean, reliable strumming technique: see page 26 for guidance**
- **The ability to understand and follow chord charts**

Chord charts are covered in more depth on pages 161-65, but the majority of progressions in this book will be shown using the chord symbols followed by a slash (/) symbol if the chord is to be repeated. For example:

$$| \ C \ / \ / \ / \ | \ G \ / \ / \ / \ |$$

This would mean the C major chord is played four times, followed by four G major chords.

FREE ACCESS on iPhone & Android etc, using any free QR code app

Scan to **HEAR** the C major chord, and access the full library of scales and chords on flametreemusic.com

START HERE

THE BASICS

I V vi IV

I IV V

ii V I

I vi IV V

BEYOND BASICS

WRITING SONGS

Chord Relationships

The harmonic links that exist between notes are central to understanding which notes will sound good together, and which won't.

The **key** of a song refers to its overall tonality, and tells you which scale will be used as the basis of the melody and which chords fit naturally into the arrangement. So, to understand a key it helps to look at its **scale**, which organizes all the notes of the key into pitch order.

The Major Scale

Different scales produce different tonalities, but they follow patterns that can be applied to each key. The patterns take the form of a set order of **tones** (whole steps) and **semitones** (half-steps). The combination of tones and semitones tells you the distance (or '**interval**') between each pitch.

By far the most important scale in music is the major scale, which always follows the same pattern:

T T S T T T S

When this pattern is applied to the key of C, it will produce the C major scale. Starting with C, a tone (**T**) up from C is D, then a tone up from D is E, then a semitone (**S**) from E is F, and so on. This produces the following notes:

C D E F G A B C

FREE ACCESS on iPhone & Android etc, using any free QR code app

Scan to **HEAR** the C major chord, and access the full library of scales and chords on flametreemusic.com

The intervals between each note and the key note are called a '2nd', a '3rd', a '4th' etc. The **quality** of that interval is dependent on the number of semitones involved. For example, in major scales there are 4 semitones between the root note and the 3rd: this is called a **major third**.

The quality of these intervals is again the same for all major scales:

C to D = Major Second

C to E = Major Third

C to F = Perfect Fourth

C to G = Perfect Fifth

C to A = Major Sixth

C to B = Major Seventh

If the interval distance is altered, this changes the tonality and overall 'status' of the interval. When 'major' intervals drop a semitone, they become 'minor'.

For example, if E here is lowered to an E♭ (from 4 to 3 semitones), its relationship to the key note is a minor 3rd. Similarly, if the major 7th lowers from the B to B♭, the interval becomes a minor 7th.

START HERE

THE BASICS

I V vi IV

I IV V

ii V I

I vi IV V

BEYOND BASICS

WRITING SONGS

FREE ACCESS on iPhone & Android etc, using any free QR code app

Scan to **HEAR** the C major chord, and access the full library of scales and chords on flametreemusic.com

START
HERE

THE
BASICS

I V vi IV

I IV V

ii V I

I vi IV V

BEYOND
BASICS

WRITING
SONGS

On the guitar, each fret is a semitone. The C major scale in standard and TAB notation looks like:

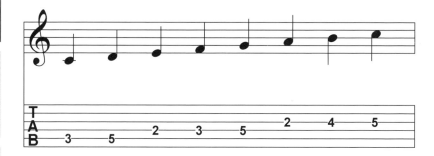

Any chords in this key are derived from these seven notes.

Chords

When a number of notes are sounded together they are called a **chord**. Chords are constructed by combining various **intervals**. Major chords, for example, are based on a major third interval.

It is common to number notes in a scale using **Roman numerals**, which refer to the note's position in the scale as well as the type of chord derived from it. An **uppercase numeral** means a chord built on that note is major; **lowercase** represents a minor chord.

So the scale of C major could be written as:

FREE ACCESS on iPhone & Android etc, using any free QR code app

Scan to **HEAR** the C major chord, and access the full library of scales and chords on flametreemusic.com

C	D	E	F	G	A	B
I	ii	iii	IV	V	vi	vii°
1st	2nd	3rd	4th	5th	6th	7th
Major	Minor	Minor	Major	Major	Minor	Diminished

START HERE

THE BASICS

I V vi IV

I IV V

ii V I

I vi IV V

BEYOND BASICS

WRITING SONGS

The 1st, 3rd and 5th notes of the major scale make up its major triad. So the C major triad contains the notes **C, E and G**.

Using the same method to form triads for each note of this major scale would give us a **harmonized** version of the C major scale. This shows us that the following chords are all within the key of C:

I:	C	(C, E, G)
ii:	Dm	(D, F, A)
iii:	Em	(E, G, B)
IV:	F	(F, A, C)
V:	G	(G, B, D)
vi:	A	(A, C, E)
vii°:	B°	(B, D, F)

On the guitar, although triads only contain three different notes, strumming three-string chords could result in quite a thin sound, so quite often chords are played with some of the notes **doubled** so that five or six strings can be strummed.

Scan to **HEAR** the C major chord, and access the full library of scales and chords on flametreemusic.com

START
HERE

THE
BASICS

I V vi IV

I IV V

ii V I

I vi IV V

BEYOND
BASICS

WRITING
SONGS

The Deconstructed Scale

Not only does a scale tell you which notes are in a key, but the position of a note in a scale also alerts you to its importance in that key.

For example, the first degree (the 'tonic') is usually central to establishing the tonality of a section of music.

The V note (the 'dominant') is also important due to its strong harmonic relationship with the tonic. So in the key of C major, G occupies an important function and position in relation to C. Another tonally important degree of the scale is the IV (the 'subdominant').

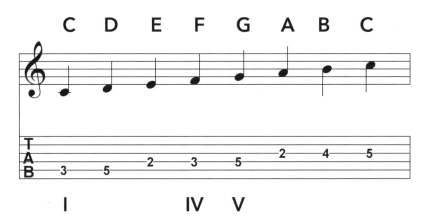

Chords built on these degrees are the key's primary chords and are the most important and definitive chords for that key. When putting together chord progressions from major scales, then, using these will establish a strong sense of key and will sound more natural.

Other useful chords in the key include the ii and vi chords, which are frequently found in chord progressions too. These most common chords are shown opposite in C, in standard and TAB notation.

FREE ACCESS on iPhone & Android
etc, using any free QR code app

Scan to **HEAR** the C major chord, and access the full library of scales and chords on flametreemusic.com

Common Chords of the C Major Scale

C Major Scale

C   D   E   F   G   A   B

I   ii   iii   IV   V   vi   vii°

START
HERE

THE
BASICS

I V vi IV

I IV V

ii V I

I vi IV V

BEYOND
BASICS

WRITING
SONGS

I – C Major

Notes: C, E, G

V – G Major

Notes: G, B, D

IV – F Major

Notes: F, A, C

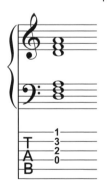

ii – D Minor

Notes: D, F, A

vi – A Minor

Notes: A, C, E

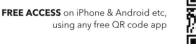

FREE ACCESS on iPhone & Android etc, using any free QR code app

Scan to **HEAR** the C major chord, and access the full library of scales and chords on flametreemusic.com

START
HERE

THE
BASICS

I V vi IV

I IV V

ii V I

I vi IV V

BEYOND
BASICS

WRITING
SONGS

Transposing to Common Keys

Scales are based on patterns on the fretboard, and can be transposed by **moving that pattern** up or down the fretboard. So once you have mastered the technique, you just need to identify what key the song is in and take it from there.

C major isn't the only key that's used in music. Other **common keys** include D major, E major, G major and A major.

All we need to do to find a major scale in another key is to apply the pattern to that starting note:

T T S T T T S

So, if this time we start on D, we would get the **D major scale**:

Scan to **HEAR** the C major chord, and access the full library of scales and chords on flametreemusic.com

Using roman numerals, you can quickly work out which are the most important chords for this key. The **I chord** would take D as its root, with the 3rd and 5th to complete the triad: D, F♯, A. The **V chord** would take G as its root, forming the triad again using notes from the scale: G, B, D.

Although there are **no fixed rules** about which chords can be combined when you are composing a song or chord progression, if you select chords from the **same key** they will always fit together well.

The following pages provide a reference for the most common chords in the most common keys.

Scan to **HEAR** the C major chord, and access the full library of scales and chords on flametreemusic.com

START
HERE

**THE
BASICS**

I V vi IV

I IV V

ii V I

I vi IV V

BEYOND
BASICS

WRITING
SONGS

START
HERE

THE
BASICS

I V vi IV

I IV V

ii V I

I vi IV V

BEYOND
BASICS

WRITING
SONGS

Common Chords of the D Major Scale

D Major Scale

D	E	F#	G	A	B	C#
I	ii	iii	IV	V	vi	vii°

I – D Major
Notes: D, F#, A

V – A Major
Notes: A, C#, E

IV – G Major
Notes: G, B, D

ii – E Minor
Notes: E, G, B

vi – B Minor
Notes: B, D, F#

FREE ACCESS on iPhone & Android
etc, using any free QR code app

Scan to **HEAR** the C major chord, and
access the full library of scales and
chords on flametreemusic.com

Common Chords of the E Major Scale

E Major Scale

E	F♯	G♯	A	B	C♯	D♯
I	ii	iii	IV	V	vi	vii°

I – E Major

Notes: E, G♯, B

V – B Major

Notes: B, D♯, F♯

IV – A Major

Notes: A, C♯, E

ii – F♯ Minor

Notes: F♯, A, C♯

vi – C♯ Minor

Notes: C♯, E, G♯

FREE ACCESS on iPhone & Android etc, using any free QR code app

Scan to **HEAR** the C major chord, and access the full library of scales and chords on flametreemusic.com

START HERE

THE BASICS

I V vi IV

I IV V

ii V I

I vi IV V

BEYOND BASICS

WRITING SONGS

START
HERE

THE
BASICS

I V vi IV

I IV V

ii V I

I vi IV V

BEYOND
BASICS

WRITING
SONGS

Common Chords of the G Major Scale

G Major Scale

G A B C D E F♯

I ii iii IV V vi vii°

I – G Major

Notes: G, B, D

V – D Major

Notes: D, F♯, A

IV – C Major

Notes: C, E, G

ii – A Minor

Notes: A, C, E

vi – E Minor

Notes: E, G, B

FREE ACCESS on iPhone & Android
etc, using any free QR code app

Scan to **HEAR** the C major chord, and
access the full library of scales and
chords on flametreemusic.com

Common Chords of the A Major Scale

A Major Scale

A B C♯ D E F♯ G♯

I ii iii IV V vi vii°

START
HERE

THE
BASICS

I V vi IV

I IV V

ii V I

I vi IV V

BEYOND
BASICS

WRITING
SONGS

I – A Major

Notes: A, C♯, E

V – E Major

Notes: E, G♯, B

IV – D Major

Notes: D, F♯, A

ii – B Minor

Notes: B, D, F♯

vi – F♯ Minor

Notes: F♯, A, C♯

FREE ACCESS on iPhone & Android etc, using any free QR code app

Scan to **HEAR** the C major chord, and access the full library of scales and chords on flametreemusic.com

25

START
HERE

THE
BASICS

I V vi IV

I IV V

ii V I

I vi IV V

BEYOND
BASICS

WRITING
SONGS

Playing the Chords

Basic Technique

Strumming

Before you can put chords together, it's essential to be at ease with strumming each chord. It will aid the **fluency** of rhythm playing if the action comes from the wrist: a fluid and easy strumming action is best achieved with the wrist loose and relaxed.

Upstrum:

Downstrum:

An upstrum should be played by an upwards movement generated from the wrist, as though the strumming hand is almost effortlessly bouncing back into position ready for the next downstrum.

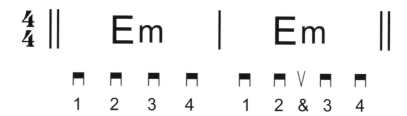

Once you've mastered the above strumming pattern, you can add another upstrum to each bar, to give one between beats two and three, and one after the fourth beat. Next, try and keep the strumming pattern going through a **chord change**, for example to A minor.

One of the best ways to practise is to play along to music that you like. Start with some easy ones at first, using mostly **open chords**. Remember, always start slow and build up speed as the movement becomes more natural.

FREE ACCESS on iPhone & Android etc, using any free QR code app

Scan to **HEAR** the C major chord, and access the full library of scales and chords on flametreemusic.com

26

Fingerpicking

An alternative to strumming, fingerpicking can add **melodic interest** to a chord progression. Many guitarists use a repetitive finger-picking pattern throughout a song to create a continuity of sound.

Each picking finger is identified by a letter:

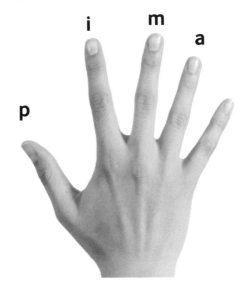

p = thumb
i = index finger
m = middle finger
a = ring finger

START HERE

THE BASICS

I V vi IV

I IV V

ii V I

Picking patterns nearly always begin by playing the root note of the chord on the bass string using the thumb. In this example, the low E string would be the first note of the pattern.

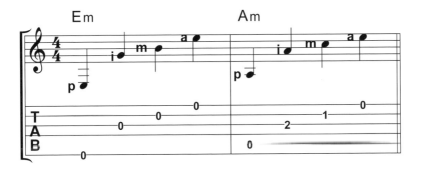

I vi IV V

BEYOND BASICS

FREE ACCESS on iPhone & Android etc, using any free QR code app

Scan to **HEAR** the C major chord, and access the full library of scales and chords on flametreemusic.com

WRITING SONGS

START
HERE

THE
BASICS

I V vi IV

I IV V

ii V I

I vi IV V

BEYOND
BASICS

WRITING
SONGS

Chord Transitions

The ability to change fluently between chord shapes without leaving any gaps in between is essential to making your chord progressions flow smoothly. There are **a few shortcuts** you can take to make your chord changes easier and faster.

Minimum Movement Principle

It's essential that chord changes are crisp, prompt, and in time. This might not be too hard when using familiar chords, but can seem daunting with chords that are new to you.

Changing between any chords, however, can be made much easier if following the '**minimum movement principle**'. This involves making only the smallest finger movement necessary between chords, and avoiding taking fingers off strings or frets only to put them back on again for the next chord.

Excess movement between chords is what slows chord changes down; the less your fingers move, the faster your chord changes will be.

Shared Notes

Always look for links, or **common notes**, between consecutive chords, so you can minimize the amount of finger movement needed when changing chords. You may be able to keep some fingers on, or at least **slide them along** a string to the next chord.

Notice the common fingering between chords in the progression opposite, in A minor: the first finger stays on the first fret and the second finger stays on the second fret throughout.

FREE ACCESS on iPhone & Android etc, using any free QR code app

Scan to **HEAR** the C major chord, and access the full library of scales and chords on flametreemusic.com

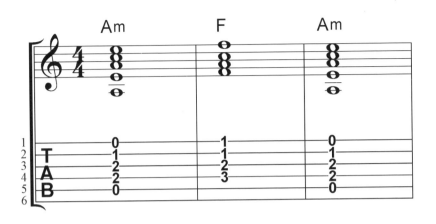

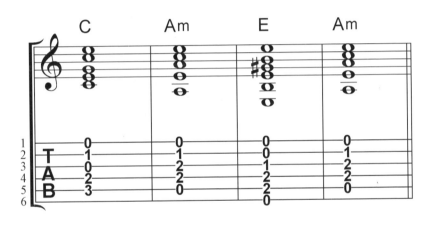

- The open position A minor and F major chords both include the note C (first fret on the B string).

- The C major chord also includes this note, and, in addition, has another note in common with the A minor chord (E on the second fret of the D string). Between Am and C only the third finger needs to be moved.

- Notice, too, how E major is the same 'shape' as Am – just on different strings.

FREE ACCESS on iPhone & Android etc, using any free QR code app

Scan to **HEAR** the C major chord, and access the full library of scales and chords on flametreemusic.com

START HERE

THE BASICS

I V vi IV

I IV V

ii V I

I vi IV V

BEYOND BASICS

WRITING SONGS

START
HERE

THE
BASICS

I V vi IV

I IV V

ii V I

I vi IV V

BEYOND
BASICS

WRITING
SONGS

'Open Vamp' Strum

If all else fails, there is a 'pro-trick' you can use that will mask any gap between chord changes: using an 'open vamp' strum.

This simply involves **strumming the open strings** while your fingers move between the chord change. While not ideal, it does mean that the overall fluency and momentum of the performance is maintained. In fact, some players actually make a feature of this technique to bring out accents within their rhythm playing.

FREE ACCESS on iPhone & Android etc, using any free QR code app

Scan to **HEAR** the C major chord, and access the full library of scales and chords on flametreemusic.com

Power Chords

In rock music, instead of full chords, abbreviated versions just using the **root and fifth note** are often played. Apart from the tone, one of the main advantages of using these 'power chords' is that it's much easier to **move quickly** from chord to chord because there are only a couple of fingers involved.

To play a fifth power chord, simply fret a note on any bass string and add a note two frets up on the adjacent higher string.

Here is the A pentatonic minor scale shown in fifths:

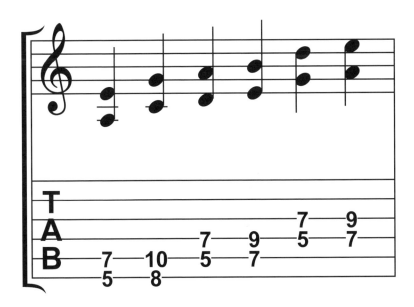

Chord diagrams for the most common power chords can be found in the Beyond Basics section on page 127.

START HERE

THE BASICS

I V vi IV

I IV V

ii V I

I vi IV V

BEYOND BASICS

WRITING SONGS

START
HERE

THE
BASICS

I V vi IV

I IV V

ii V I

I vi IV V

BEYOND
BASICS

WRITING
SONGS

Sliding Chords

The guitar is one of the few instruments on which you can slide chords up and down, changing their pitch easily and smoothly. The technique creates a fluidity and smoothness of sound, and forms a core component of rhythm-guitarist's technique in nearly all musical styles.

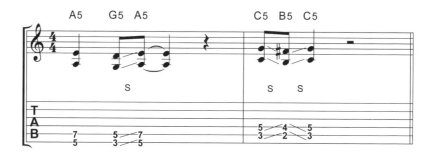

When sliding chords it's important to ensure that the chord shape is maintained, so that one finger doesn't end up a fret ahead of the rest. Keep the chord shape under control, whilst keeping the fingers relaxed enough to slide up or down the fretboard.

- **Look for any links between the different chord fingerings**
- **Place the fingers for each complete chord shape on the fretboard together**
- **Practise very slowly so that you don't develop a habit of slowing down or stopping between chord changes**

For more information about the **I vi ii V** chord progression opposite, see pages 114-15.

FREE ACCESS on iPhone & Android etc, using any free QR code app

Scan to **HEAR** the C major chord, and access the full library of scales and chords on flametreemusic.com

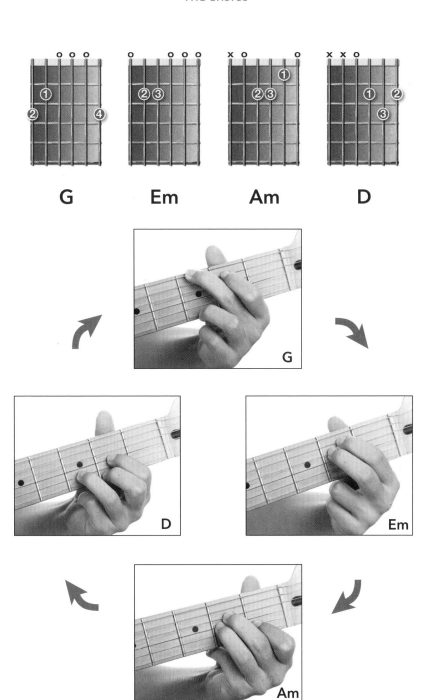

G   Em   Am   D

START HERE

THE BASICS

I V vi IV

I IV V

ii V I

I vi IV V

BEYOND BASICS

WRITING SONGS

FREE ACCESS on iPhone & Android etc, using any free QR code app

Scan to **HEAR** the C major chord, and access the full library of scales and chords on flametreemusic.com

START
HERE

THE
BASICS

I V vi IV

I IV V

ii V I

I vi IV V

BEYOND
BASICS

WRITING
SONGS

Types of Chord Progression

Chord progressions can take various forms, to the point where they can sound and feel very different from each other, even when using the same chords.

The Beyond Basics section of this book covers further embellishments and structural techniques that can be used to make a progression sound more interesting, but here is a quick outline of the different types of progression you might come across.

Length

One of the most obvious ways in which chord progressions can differ is in their length. It's very common for progressions to involve **four chords** before the sequence repeats, as in the case of the first progression in this book: **I V vi IV**. This gives a very comfortable structure for standard timing: four chords, each lasting four beats.

A progression can be as long or short as you like though. For example, the **ii V I** is a popular three-chord progression, and the **twelve-bar blues progression** is a famous longer sequence that is still very recognizable.

You can play around with the length of the progressions in this book to hear what sounds best. You may wish, for example, to lengthen the **ii V I** into a four-chord setup by beginning the progression with the I chord.

FREE ACCESS on iPhone & Android etc, using any free QR code app

Scan to **HEAR** the C major chord, and access the full library of scales and chords on flametreemusic.com

Also worth considering in relation to length is how **frequently** the chords change within them. If you're not sure what to try, it's generally best to change chord on the first beat of each measure, as this gives a strong sense of rhythm. But it's possible to change more or less frequently than that: there can be a chord change every beat, or every two beats, or every two bars, or on the third beat of each measure, and so on.

Major/Minor

The main four progressions shown in this book all take their chords from **major scales**, as this is the most common and simplest type of scale to use. It's possible to use other types of scales as the basis for making your own progression though.

For example, one of the minor scales could be used to generate a different combination of chords in the key. See pages 140-41 for details on using a different scale to build progressions.

Style

The way that chords in a progression are styled can give the music its **identity**. This is to the extent that the same chord progression could be played in such a way as to sound very different to another song using the same chord progression.

Once you've mastered the basic chords involved, there are many **melodic and rhythmic techniques** you can incorporate into your progression to add some variety.

Tips for styling your progressions can be found in the Writing Songs section of this book.

START
HERE

THE
BASICS

I V vi IV

I IV V

ii V I

I vi IV V

BEYOND
BASICS

WRITING
SONGS

FREE ACCESS on iPhone & Android etc, using any free QR code app

Scan to **HEAR** the C major chord, and access the full library of scales and chords on flametreemusic.com

START
HERE

THE
BASICS

I V vi IV

I V vi IV

This incredibly popular chord progression can be found in many of the songs heard today. The following pages will give the chord names and diagrams for this progression in the key of C major, and then in the other common keys of D major, E major, G major and A major.

While that this is the most common organization of the chords, the same four chords can be used in a different order (see the variations on pages 52–55, and the alternative main progression on pages 96–113).

I IV V

This section will cover:

ii V I

- How I V vi IV relates to keys and scales
- I V vi IV shown in practice in the key of C
- I V vi IV transposed to other common keys: D, E, G and A

I vi IV V

- Examples of I V vi IV in action
- Quick reference page of I V vi IV in the common keys
- Two variations of the progression to try out
- Clear chord names, chord diagrams and QR code links throughout

BEYOND
BASICS

WRITING
SONGS

FREE ACCESS on iPhone & Android etc, using any free QR code app

Scan to **HEAR** the C major chord, and access the full library of scales and chords on flametreemusic.com

START
HERE

THE
BASICS

I V vi IV

I IV V

ii V I

I vi IV V

BEYOND
BASICS

WRITING
SONGS

FREE ACCESS on iPhone & Android etc, using any free QR code app

Scan to **HEAR** the C major chord, and access the full library of scales and chords on flametreemusic.com

START
HERE

THE
BASICS

I V vi IV

I IV V

ii V I

I vi IV V

BEYOND
BASICS

WRITING
SONGS

I V vi IV
in C

In C major, the chords needed for the **I V vi IV** progression are formed using the notes of the C major scale:

C	D	E	F	G	A	B
I	ii	iii	IV	V	vi	vii°

So the chords for this progression in C major are:

C	G	Am	F
I	V	vi	IV
C major	G major	A minor	F major

In a standard 4/4 song, with four beats per bar, these are the chords you would play:

C / / /
G / / /
Am / / /
F / / /

FREE ACCESS on iPhone & Android etc, using any free QR code app

Scan to **HEAR** the C major chord, and access the full library of scales and chords on flametreemusic.com

C major
Chord Spelling
1st (C), 3rd (E), 5th (G)

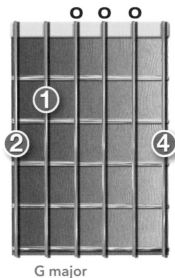

G major
Chord Spelling
1st (G), 3rd (B), 5th (D)

A minor
Chord Spelling
1st (A), ♭3rd (C), 5th (E)

F major
Chord Spelling
1st (F), 3rd (A), 5th (C)

START HERE

THE BASICS

I V vi IV

I IV V

ii V I

I vi IV V

BEYOND BASICS

WRITING SONGS

FREE ACCESS on iPhone & Android etc, using any free QR code app

Scan to **HEAR** the C major chord, and access the full library of scales and chords on flametreemusic.com

Other Keys
I V vi IV in D

In D major, the chords needed for the **I V vi IV** progression are formed using the notes of the D major scale:

D	E	F♯	G	A	B	C♯
I	ii	iii	IV	V	vi	vii°

So the chords for this progression in D major are:

D	A	Bm	G
I	V	vi	IV
D major	A major	B minor	G major

In a standard 4/4 song, with four beats per bar, these are the chords you would play:

D / / /

A / / /

Bm / / /

G / / /

Scan to **HEAR** the C major chord, and access the full library of scales and chords on flametreemusic.com

START HERE

THE BASICS

I V vi IV

I IV V

ii V I

I vi IV V

BEYOND BASICS

WRITING SONGS

D major
Chord Spelling

1st (D), 3rd (F#), 5th (A)

A major
Chord Spelling

1st (A), 3rd (C#), 5th (E)

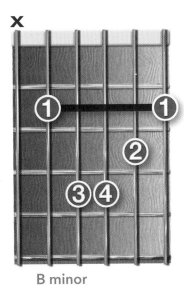

B minor
Chord Spelling

1st (B), b3rd (D), 5th (F#)

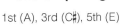

G major
Chord Spelling

1st (G), 3rd (B), 5th (D)

START HERE

THE BASICS

I V vi IV

I IV V

ii V I

I vi IV V

BEYOND BASICS

WRITING SONGS

FREE ACCESS on iPhone & Android etc, using any free QR code app

Scan to **HEAR** the C major chord, and access the full library of scales and chords on flametreemusic.com

START
HERE

THE
BASICS

I V vi IV

I IV V

ii V I

I vi IV V

BEYOND
BASICS

WRITING
SONGS

Other Keys
I V vi IV in E

In E major, the chords needed for the **I V vi IV** progression are formed using the notes of the E major scale:

E	F♯	G♯	A	B	C♯	D♯
I	ii	iii	IV	V	vi	vii°

So the chords for this progression in E major are:

E	B	C♯m	A
I	V	vi	IV
E major	B major	C♯ minor	A major

In a standard 4/4 song, with four beats per bar, these are the chords you would play:

E	/	/	/
B	/	/	/
C♯m	/	/	/
A	/	/	/

FREE ACCESS on iPhone & Android
etc, using any free QR code app

Scan to **HEAR** the C major chord, and access the full library of scales and chords on flametreemusic.com

E major
Chord Spelling
1st (E), 3rd (G#), 5th (B)

B major
Chord Spelling
1st (B), 3rd (D#), 5th (F#)

C# minor
Chord Spelling
1st (C#), b3rd (E), 5th (G#)

A major
Chord Spelling
1st (A), 3rd (C#), 5th (E)

START
HERE

THE
BASICS

I V vi IV

I IV V

ii V I

I vi IV V

BEYOND
BASICS

WRITING
SONGS

FREE ACCESS on iPhone & Android etc,
using any free QR code app

Scan to **HEAR** the C major chord, and
access the full library of scales and
chords on flametreemusic.com

START HERE

THE BASICS

I V vi IV

I IV V

ii V I

I vi IV V

BEYOND BASICS

WRITING SONGS

Other Keys
I V vi IV in G

In G major, the chords needed for the **I V vi IV** progression are formed using the notes of the G major scale:

G	A	B	C	D	E	F#
I	ii	iii	IV	V	vi	vii°

So the chords for this progression in G major are:

G	D	Em	C
I	V	vi	IV
G major	D major	E minor	C major

In a standard 4/4 song, with four beats per bar, these are the chords you would play:

G / / /

D / / /

Em / / /

C / / /

Scan to **HEAR** the C major chord, and access the full library of scales and chords on flametreemusic.com

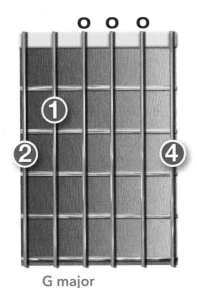

G major
Chord Spelling
1st (G), 3rd (B), 5th (D)

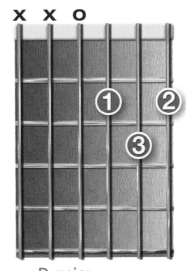

D major
Chord Spelling
1st (D), 3rd (F#), 5th (A)

E minor
Chord Spelling
1st (E), ♭3rd (G), 5th (B)

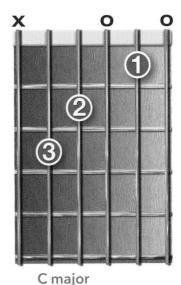

C major
Chord Spelling
1st (C), 3rd (E), 5th (G)

START HERE

THE BASICS

I V vi IV

I IV V

ii V I

I vi IV V

BEYOND BASICS

WRITING SONGS

FREE ACCESS on iPhone & Android etc, using any free QR code app

Scan to **HEAR** the C major chord, and access the full library of scales and chords on flametreemusic.com

START
HERE

THE
BASICS

I V vi IV

I IV V

ii V I

I vi IV V

BEYOND
BASICS

WRITING
SONGS

Other Keys
I V vi IV in A

In A major, the chords needed for the **I V vi IV** progression are formed using the notes of the A major scale:

A	B	C♯	D	E	F♯	G♯
I	ii	iii	IV	V	vi	vii°

So the chords for this progression in A major are:

A	E	F♯m	D
I	V	vi	IV
A major	E major	F♯ minor	D major

In a standard 4/4 song, with four beats per bar, these are the chords you would play:

A   /   /   /
E   /   /   /
F♯m /   /   /
D   /   /   /

Scan to **HEAR** the C major chord, and access the full library of scales and chords on flametreemusic.com

A major

Chord Spelling

1st (A), 3rd (C♯), 5th (E)

E major

Chord Spelling

1st (E), 3rd (G♯), 5th (B)

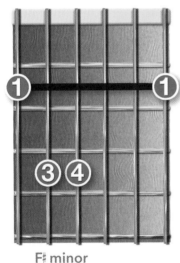

F♯ minor

Chord Spelling

1st (F♯), ♭3rd (A), 5th (C♯)

D major

Chord Spelling

1st (D), 3rd (F♯), 5th (A)

START HERE

THE BASICS

I V vi IV

I IV V

ii V I

I vi IV V

BEYOND BASICS

WRITING SONGS

Examples

Below is a list of songs that use the **I V vi IV** sequence of chords, with the majority being in C major. This is just a small selection of the many current songs that favour this popular chord progression.

Grenade – Bruno Mars

No Woman No Cry – Bob Marley

Let It Be – The Beatles

So Lonely – The Police

Poker Face – Lady Gaga

Imagine – John Lennon

House of the Rising Sun – The Animals

Stay – Rihanna

Hallelujah – Leonard Cohen

Heartbreaker – Mariah Carey/Jay-Z

I Believe I Can Fly – R. Kelly

I Write Sins Not Tragedies – Panic! At the Disco

Stay with Me – Sam Smith

School – Nirvana

Don't Look Back in Anger – Oasis

Lovesong – The Cure

Love Yourself – Justin Bieber

Demons – Imagine Dragons

Photograph – Ed Sheeran

Under the Bridge – Red Hot Chili Peppers

She Will Be Loved – Maroon 5

Price Tag – Jessie J

Opposite are a couple of examples of the **I V vi IV** progression in use, both in C major. In the first, the accompanying chords change twice per bar. In the second example, the progression leads back to a final V (G) chord.

FREE ACCESS on iPhone & Android etc, using any free QR code app

Scan to **HEAR** the C major chord, and access the full library of scales and chords on flametreemusic.com

Song 1

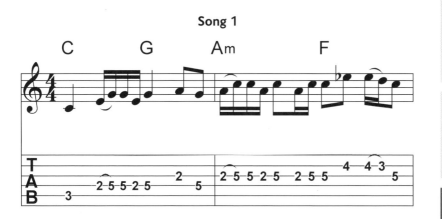

START
HERE

THE
BASICS

I V vi IV

I IV V

ii V I

I vi IV V

BEYOND
BASICS

WRITING
SONGS

Song 2

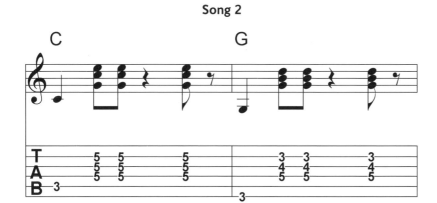

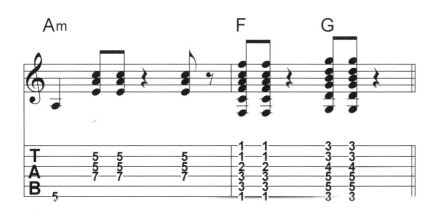

FREE ACCESS on iPhone & Android etc,
using any free QR code app

Scan to **HEAR** the C major chord, and
access the full library of scales and
chords on flametreemusic.com

Quick Reference

Here's an at-a-glance list of the I V vi IV progression in the most common keys, as covered in the previous pages.

START HERE

THE BASICS

I V vi IV

I IV V

ii V I

I vi IV V

BEYOND BASICS

WRITING SONGS

C Major

C	G	Am	F
I	V	vi	IV
1st	5th	6th minor	4th

D Major

D	A	Bm	G
I	V	vi	IV
1st	5th	6th minor	4th

E Major

E	B	C#m	A
I	V	vi	IV
1st	5th	6th minor	4th

G Major

G	D	Em	C
I	V	vi	IV
1st	5th	6th minor	4th

A Major

A	E	F#m	D
I	V	vi	IV
1st	5th	6th minor	4th

FREE ACCESS on iPhone & Android etc, using any free QR code app

Scan to **HEAR** the C major chord, and access the full library of scales and chords on flametreemusic.com

START
HERE

THE
BASICS

I V vi IV

I IV V

ii V I

I vi IV V

BEYOND
BASICS

WRITING
SONGS

FREE ACCESS on iPhone & Android etc, using any free QR code app

Scan to **HEAR** the C major chord, and access the full library of scales and chords on flametreemusic.com

Variations

The four chords in the **I V vi IV** progression can be used in a number of different combinations. Some of the most popular rearrangements of the chords include **vi IV I V**, and **I IV vi V**. The following pages will briefly show these progressions laid out for C major, so you can play around with them to see which progression works best for you. If you want to use them in other keys they can be transposed in the same way as has been shown previously.

vi IV I V

Again, use the major scale of the key you're in to work out which chords are needed for this progression. In C major:

C	D	E	F	G	A	B
I	ii	iii	IV	V	vi	vii°

So the chords for this progression in C major are:

Am	F	C	G
vi	IV	I	V
A minor	F major	C major	G major

FREE ACCESS on iPhone & Android etc, using any free QR code app

Scan to **HEAR** the C major chord, and access the full library of scales and chords on flametreemusic.com

A minor
Chord Spelling
1st (A), ♭3rd (C), 5th (E)

F major
Chord Spelling
1st (F), 3rd (A), 5th (C)

C major
Chord Spelling
1st (C), 3rd (E), 5th (G)

G major
Chord Spelling
1st (G), 3rd (B), 5th (D)

Scan to **HEAR** the C major chord, and access the full library of scales and chords on flametreemusic.com

START HERE

THE BASICS

I V vi IV

I IV V

ii V I

I vi IV V

BEYOND BASICS

WRITING SONGS

START
HERE

THE
BASICS

I V vi IV

I IV V

ii V I

I vi IV V

BEYOND
BASICS

WRITING
SONGS

I IV vi V

This progression is another variation of the same four chords. This one switches the position of the IV and V chords, so you can just use the examples on pages 38–47 taking care to swap those two chords round if you want to try this variation.

If you're working from scratch though, the major scale of the key you're in will show you which chords are needed for this progression. In C major:

C	D	E	F	G	A	B
I	ii	iii	IV	V	vi	vii°

So the chords for this progression in C major are:

C	F	Am	G
I	IV	vi	V
C major	F major	A minor	G major

Scan to **HEAR** the C major chord, and access the full library of scales and chords on flametreemusic.com

C major

Chord Spelling

1st (C), 3rd (E), 5th (G)

F major

Chord Spelling

1st (F), 3rd (A), 5th (C)

A minor

Chord Spelling

1st (A), ♭3rd (C), 5th (E)

G major

Chord Spelling

1st (G), 3rd (B), 5th (D)

Scan to **HEAR** the C major chord, and access the full library of scales and chords on flametreemusic.com

START HERE

THE BASICS

I V vi IV

I IV V

ii V I

I vi IV V

BEYOND BASICS

WRITING SONGS

START
HERE

THE
BASICS

I V vi IV

I IV V

ii V I

I vi IV V

BEYOND
BASICS

WRITING
SONGS

I IV V

Another very common chord progression is the I IV V. It uses the 'primary chords' of a key, which are frequently used because of their strong harmonic links with one another. In Blues music, the same chord progression is used to great effect with dominant 7th chords instead of the basic triads.

The names, spellings, diagrams and QR code links for the chords in this progression are given in the following pages, for the key of C and other popular major keys.

This section will cover:

- How I IV V relates to keys and scales
- I IV V shown in practice in the key of C
- I IV V transposed to other common keys: D, E, G and A
- Examples of I IV V in action
- Quick reference page of I IV V in the common keys
- Two variations of the progression to try out
- Clear chord names, chord diagrams and QR code links throughout

FREE ACCESS on iPhone & Android etc, using any free QR code app

Scan to **HEAR** the C major chord, and access the full library of scales and chords on flametreemusic.com

START
HERE

THE
BASICS

I V vi IV

I IV V

ii V I

I vi IV V

BEYOND
BASICS

WRITING
SONGS

FREE ACCESS on iPhone & Android etc, using any free QR code app

Scan to **HEAR** the C major chord, and access the full library of scales and chords on flametreemusic.com

START
HERE

THE
BASICS

I V vi IV

I IV V

ii V I

I vi IV V

BEYOND
BASICS

WRITING
SONGS

I IV V
in C

In C major, the chords needed for the **I IV V** progression are formed using the notes of the C major scale:

C	D	E	F	G	A	B
I	ii	iii	IV	V	vi	vii°

So the chords for this progression in C major are:

C	F	G
I	IV	V
C major	F major	G major

In a standard 4/4 song, with four beats per bar, these are the chords you would play:

C / / /
F / / /
G / / /

Scan to **HEAR** the C major chord, and access the full library of scales and chords on flametreemusic.com

X   O   O

C major

Chord Spelling

1st (C), 3rd (E), 5th (G)

X   X

F major

Chord Spelling

1st (F), 3rd (A), 5th (C)

O   O   O

G major

Chord Spolling

1st (G), 3rd (B), 5th (D)

START HERE

THE BASICS

I V vi IV

I IV V

ii V I

I vi IV V

BEYOND BASICS

WRITING SONGS

FREE ACCESS on iPhone & Android etc, using any free QR code app

Scan to **HEAR** the C major chord, and access the full library of scales and chords on flametreemusic.com

Other Keys
I IV V in D

In D major, the chords needed for the **I IV V** progression are formed using the notes of the D major scale:

D   E   F♯   G   A   B   C♯

I   ii   iii   IV   V   vi   vii°

So the chords for this progression in D major are:

D   G   A

I   IV   V

D major   G major   A major

In a standard 4/4 song, with four beats per bar, these are the chords you would play:

D / / /
G / / /
A / / /

Scan to **HEAR** the C major chord, and access the full library of scales and chords on flametreemusic.com

D major
Chord Spelling
1st (D), 3rd (F♯), 5th (A)

G major
Chord Spelling
1st (G), 3rd (B), 5th (D)

START HERE

THE BASICS

I V vi IV

I IV V

ii V I

I vi IV V

BEYOND BASICS

WRITING SONGS

A major
Chord Spelling
1st (A), 3rd (C♯), 5th (E)

FREE ACCESS on iPhone & Android etc, using any free QR code app

Scan to **HEAR** the C major chord, and access the full library of scales and chords on flametreemusic.com

Other Keys
I IV V in E

In E major, the chords needed for the **I IV V** progression are formed using the notes of the E major scale:

E	F♯	G♯	A	B	C♯	D♯
I	ii	iii	IV	V	vi	vii°

So the chords for this progression in E major are:

E	A	B
I	IV	V
E major	A major	B major

In a standard 4/4 song, with four beats per bar, these are the chords you would play:

E	/	/	/
A	/	/	/
B	/	/	/

Scan to **HEAR** the C major chord, and access the full library of scales and chords on flametreemusic.com

Sidebar navigation:
START HERE
THE BASICS
I V vi IV
I IV V
ii V I
I vi IV V
BEYOND BASICS
WRITING SONGS

E major

Chord Spelling

1st (E), 3rd (G♯), 5th (B)

A major

Chord Spelling

1st (A), 3rd (C♯), 5th (E)

B major

Chord Spelling

1st (B), 3rd (D♯), 5th (F♯)

START HERE

THE BASICS

I V vi IV

I IV V

ii V I

I vi IV V

BEYOND BASICS

WRITING SONGS

Other Keys
I IV V in G

In G major, the chords needed for the **I IV V** progression are formed using the notes of the G major scale:

G	A	B	C	D	E	F♯
I	ii	iii	IV	V	vi	vii°

So the chords for this progression in G major are:

G	C	D
I	IV	V
G major	C major	D major

In a standard 4/4 song, with four beats per bar, these are the chords you would play:

G / / /
C / / /
D / / /

Scan to **HEAR** the C major chord, and access the full library of scales and chords on flametreemusic.com

START HERE

THE BASICS

I V vi IV

I IV V

ii V I

I vi IV V

BEYOND BASICS

WRITING SONGS

G major

Chord Spelling

1st (G), 3rd (B), 5th (D)

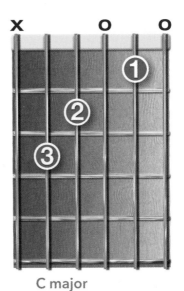

C major

Chord Spelling

1st (C), 3rd (E), 5th (G)

D major

Chord Spelling

1st (D), 3rd (F♯), 5th (A)

Scan to **HEAR** the C major chord, and access the full library of scales and chords on flametreemusic.com

START HERE

THE BASICS

I V vi IV

I IV V

ii V I

I vi IV V

BEYOND BASICS

WRITING SONGS

Other Keys
I IV V in A

In A major, the chords needed for the **I IV V** progression are formed using the notes of the A major scale:

A	B	C♯	D	E	F♯	G♯
I	ii	iii	IV	V	vi	vii°

So the chords for this progression in A major are:

A	D	E
I	IV	V
A major	D major	E major

In a standard 4/4 song, with four beats per bar, these are the chords you would play:

A / / /
D / / /
E / / /

FREE ACCESS on iPhone & Android
etc, using any free QR code app

Scan to **HEAR** the C major chord, and access the full library of scales and chords on flametreemusic.com

A major

Chord Spelling

1st (A), 3rd (C#), 5th (E)

D major

Chord Spelling

1st (D), 3rd (F#), 5th (A)

E major

Chord Spelling

1st (E), 3rd (G#), 5th (B)

START HERE

THE BASICS

I V vi IV

I IV V

ii V I

I vi IV V

BEYOND BASICS

WRITING SONGS

FREE ACCESS on iPhone & Android etc, using any free QR code app

Scan to **HEAR** the C major chord, and access the full library of scales and chords on flametreemusic.com

Examples

Below is a list of songs that use the **I IV V** progression in some form or other, including the twelve-bar blues.

Johnny B. Goode – Chuck Berry
Blue Suede Shoes – Carl Perkins
Wild Thing – The Troggs
Bad Moon Rising – Creedance Clearwater Revival
Good Riddance – Green Day
Mustang Sally – The Commitments/Wilson Pickett
Rock and Roll – Led Zeppelin
Should I Stay or Should I Go – The Clash
Folsom Prison Blues – Johnny Cash
That's Not My Name – The Ting Tings
Walking by Myself – Gary Moore
Great Balls of Fire – Jerry Lee Lewis
Rock Around the Clock – Max C. Freedman and James E. Myers

Opposite are two examples of **I IV V** in action.

The first is in **C major**, using C, F and G chords.

The second example in **E major** uses 7th chords and ends on the strong E major chord, using the progression: **Imaj7 IVmaj7 Vsus4 V7 I.**

START HERE

THE BASICS

I V vi IV

I IV V

ii V I

I vi IV V

BEYOND BASICS

WRITING SONGS

FREE ACCESS on iPhone & Android etc, using any free QR code app

Scan to **HEAR** the C major chord, and access the full library of scales and chords on flametreemusic.com

Song 1

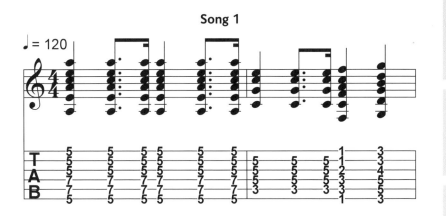

Song 2

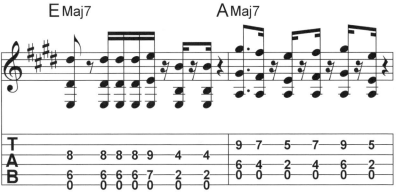

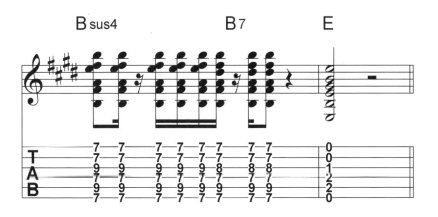

START HERE

THE BASICS

I V vi IV

I IV V

ii V I

I vi IV V

BEYOND BASICS

WRITING SONGS

FREE ACCESS on iPhone & Android etc, using any free QR code app

Scan to **HEAR** the C major chord, and access the full library of scales and chords on flametreemusic.com

START
HERE

THE
BASICS

I V vi IV

I IV V

ii V I

I vi IV V

BEYOND
BASICS

WRITING
SONGS

Quick Reference

Here's an at-a-glance list of the **I   IV   V** progression in the most common keys, as covered in the previous pages.

C Major

C	F	G
I	IV	V
1st	4th	5th

D Major

D	G	A
I	IV	V
1st	4th	5th

E Major

E	A	B
I	IV	V
1st	4th	5th

G Major

G	C	D
I	IV	V
1st	4th	5th

A Major

A	D	E
I	IV	V
1st	4th	5th

FREE ACCESS on iPhone & Android etc, using any free QR code app

Scan to **HEAR** the C major chord, and access the full library of scales and chords on flametreemusic.com

START
HERE

THE
BASICS

I V vi IV

I IV V

ii V I

I vi IV V

BEYOND
BASICS

WRITING
SONGS

FREE ACCESS on iPhone & Android etc, using any free QR code app

Scan to **HEAR** the C major chord, and access the full library of scales and chords on flametreemusic.com

START
HERE

THE
BASICS

I V vi IV

I IV V

ii V I

I vi IV V

BEYOND
BASICS

WRITING
SONGS

Variations

The 'twelve-bar blues' is a common version of the **I   IV   V** progression, and it is also common for the basic chords to incorporate dominant 7ths. The variations here are given in C major, though can be transposed to any key using the techniques described in the previous sections.

Adding 7ths: I7 IV7 V7

A straightforward popular version of the **I   IV   V** progression using 7ths would be for all three chords to be in their **dominant 7th** forms. A dominant 7th chord uses the same major triad, but with an added **flattened 7th.**

As we already know the chords for I IV V in C major, we can use their relevant scales to find the 'seventh' note for C, F, and G:

C	D	E	F	G	A	B
F	G	A	B♭	C	D	E
G	A	B	C	D	E	F♯
I	ii	iii	IV	V	vi	vii°

So adding a flattened 7th to each of the chords gives us:

I	=	C	(C, E, G)
I7	**=**	**C7**	**(C, E, G, B♭)**
IV	=	F	(F, A, C)
IV7	**=**	**F7**	**(F, A, C, E♭)**
V	=	G	(G, B, D)
V7	**=**	**G7**	**(G, B, D, F)**

V7 chords in particular are very popular in blues music. They're quite easy to spot as all the notes in the chord can also be found in the major scale: here, all the notes in G7 can be found in the C major scale.

FREE ACCESS on iPhone & Android etc, using any free QR code app

Scan to **HEAR** the C major chord, and access the full library of scales and chords on flametreemusic.com

C7

Chord Spelling

1st (C), 3rd (E), 5th (G), ♭7th (B♭)

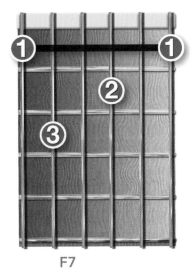

F7

Chord Spelling

1st (F), 3rd (A), 5th (C), ♭7th (E♭)

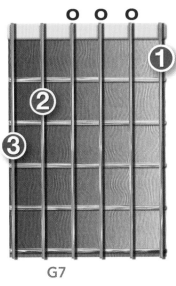

G7

Chord Spelling

1st (G), 3rd (B), 5th (D), ♭7th (F)

START
HERE

THE
BASICS

I V vi IV

I IV V

ii V I

I vi IV V

BEYOND
BASICS

WRITING
SONGS

FREE ACCESS on iPhone & Android etc, using any free QR code app

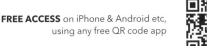

Scan to **HEAR** the C major chord, and access the full library of scales and chords on flametreemusic.com

START
HERE

THE
BASICS

I V vi IV

I IV V

ii V I

I vi IV V

BEYOND
BASICS

WRITING
SONGS

The Twelve-bar Blues

Perhaps most famously, the **I   IV   V** progression forms the basis of the twelve-bar blues. This can take various forms, but a typical example is laid out below:

I	I	I	I
IV	IV	I	I
V	IV	I	I

Using the scale of C major, we can see how this translates into the key of C:

C	D	E	F	G	A	B
I	ii	iii	IV	V	vi	vii°

So with four beats per bar, these are the chords you would play in C major:

C	C	C	C
F	F	C	C
G	F	C	C

The chord diagrams opposite show this C major twelve-bar blues progression in its basic form. It's common to use 7ths here too, so play around with using the **I7, IV7 and V7** variants to get the effect you want.

See page 119 for more chord diagrams of common 7th chords.

START
HERE

THE
BASICS

I V vi IV

I IV V

ii V I

I vi IV V

BEYOND
BASICS

WRITING
SONGS

C major

C major

C major

C major

F major

F major

C major

C major

G major

F major

C major

C major

FREE ACCESS on iPhone & Android etc, using any free QR code app

Scan to **HEAR** the C major chord, and access the full library of scales and chords on flametreemusic.com

75

START
HERE

THE
BASICS

I V vi IV

I IV V

ii V I

I vi IV V

BEYOND
BASICS

WRITING
SONGS

ii V I

The third main chord progression you're likely to come across in lots of music is the **ii V I**. A popular feature in Jazz music, this three-chord progression contains the satisfying V to I chord movement, which feels natural and pleasing to the ear, especially at the end of a section.

Like all the other progressions in this book, **ii V I** can easily be transposed between keys, and the following pages show examples in C major, D major, E major, G major, A major and A minor.

This section will cover:

- **How ii V I relates to keys and scales**
- **ii V I shown in practice in the key of C**
- **ii V I transposed to other common keys:**
  D, E, G and A
- **Examples of ii V I in action**
- **Quick reference page of ii V I in the common keys**
- **Two variations of the progression to try out**
- **Clear chord names, chord diagrams and QR code**
  links throughout

FREE ACCESS on iPhone & Android etc, using any free QR code app

Scan to **HEAR** the C major chord, and access the full library of scales and chords on flametreemusic.com

START
HERE

THE
BASICS

I V vi IV

I IV V

ii V I

I vi IV V

BEYOND
BASICS

WRITING
SONGS

FREE ACCESS on iPhone & Android etc, using any free QR code app

Scan to **HEAR** the C major chord, and access the full library of scales and chords on flametreemusic.com

ii V I
in C

In C major, the chords needed for the **ii V I** progression are formed using the notes of the C major scale:

C D E F G A B

I ii iii IV V vi vii°

So the chords for this progression in C major are:

Dm G C

ii V I

D minor G major C major

In a standard 4/4 song, with four beats per bar, these are the chords you would play:

Dm / / /
G / / /
C / / /

FREE ACCESS on iPhone & Android etc, using any free QR code app

Scan to **HEAR** the C major chord, and access the full library of scales and chords on flametreemusic.com

D minor
Chord Spelling
1st (D), ♭3rd (F), 5th (A)

G major
Chord Spelling
1st (G), 3rd (B), 5th (D)

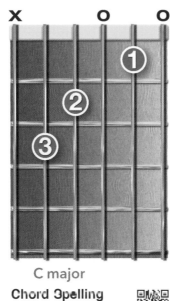

C major
Chord Spelling
1st (C), 3rd (E), 5th (G)

FREE ACCESS on iPhone & Android etc, using any free QR code app

Scan to **HEAR** the C major chord, and access the full library of scales and chords on flametreemusic.com

START HERE

THE BASICS

I V vi IV

I IV V

ii V I

I vi IV V

BEYOND BASICS

WRITING SONGS

START
HERE

THE
BASICS

I V vi IV

I IV V

ii V I

I vi IV V

BEYOND
BASICS

WRITING
SONGS

Other Keys
ii V I in D

In D major, the chords needed for the **ii V I** progression are formed using the notes of the D major scale:

D E F♯ G A B C♯

I ii iii IV V vi vii°

So the chords for this progression in D major are:

Em A D

ii V I

E minor A major D major

In a standard 4/4 song, with four beats per bar, these are the chords you would play:

Em / / /
A / / /
D / / /

FREE ACCESS on iPhone & Android etc, using any free QR code app

Scan to **HEAR** the C major chord, and access the full library of scales and chords on flametreemusic.com

E minor

Chord Spelling

1st (E), ♭3rd (G), 5th (B)

A major

Chord Spelling

1st (A), 3rd (C♯), 5th (E)

START
HERE

THE
BASICS

I V vi IV

I IV V

ii V I

I vi IV V

BEYOND
BASICS

WRITING
SONGS

D major

Chord Spelling

1st (D), 3rd (F♯), 5th (A)

FREE ACCESS on iPhone & Android etc, using any free QR code app

Scan to **HEAR** the C major chord, and access the full library of scales and chords on flametreemusic.com

START
HERE

THE
BASICS

I V vi IV

I IV V

ii V I

I vi IV V

BEYOND
BASICS

WRITING
SONGS

Other Keys
ii V I in E

In E major, the chords needed for the **ii V I** progression are formed using the notes of the E major scale:

E	F♯	G♯	A	B	C♯	D♯
I	ii	iii	IV	V	vi	vii°

So the chords for this progression in E major are:

F♯m	B	E
ii	V	I
F♯ minor	B major	E major

In a standard 4/4 song, with four beats per bar, these are the chords you would play:

F♯m /   /   /

B   /   /   /

E   /   /   /

Scan to **HEAR** the C major chord, and access the full library of scales and chords on flametreemusic.com

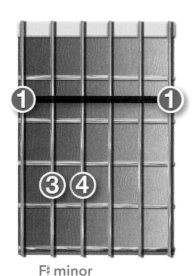

F♯ minor

Chord Spelling

1st (F♯), ♭3rd (A), 5th (C♯)

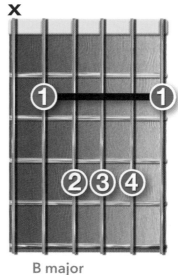

B major

Chord Spelling

1st (B), 3rd (D♯), 5th (F♯)

E major

Chord Spelling

1st (E), 3rd (G♯), 5th (B)

START HERE

THE BASICS

I V vi IV

I IV V

ii V I

I vi IV V

BEYOND BASICS

WRITING SONGS

Other Keys
ii V I in G

In G major, the chords needed for the **ii V I** progression are formed using the notes of the G major scale:

G	A	B	C	D	E	F#
I	ii	iii	IV	V	vi	vii°

So the chords for this progression in G major are:

Am	D	G
ii	V	I
A minor	D major	G major

In a standard 4/4 song, with four beats per bar, these are the chords you would play:

Am /   /   /

D   /   /   /

G   /   /   /

FREE ACCESS on iPhone & Android etc, using any free QR code app

Scan to **HEAR** the C major chord, and access the full library of scales and chords on flametreemusic.com

A minor

Chord Spelling

1st (A), ♭3rd (C), 5th (E)

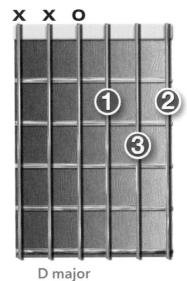

D major

Chord Spelling

1st (D), 3rd (F♯), 5th (A)

G major

Chord Spelling

1st (G), 3rd (B), 5th (D)

START HERE

THE BASICS

I V vi IV

I IV V

ii V I

I vi IV V

BEYOND BASICS

WRITING SONGS

FREE ACCESS on iPhone & Android etc, using any free QR code app

Scan to **HEAR** the C major chord, and access the full library of scales and chords on flametreemusic.com

Other Keys
ii V I in A

In A major, the chords needed for the **ii V I** progression are formed using the notes of the A major scale:

A	B	C♯	D	E	F♯	G♯
I	ii	iii	IV	V	vi	vii°

So the chords for this progression in A major are:

Bm	E	A
ii	V	I
B minor	E major	A major

In a standard 4/4 song, with four beats per bar, these are the chords you would play:

Bm	/	/	/
E	/	/	/
A	/	/	/

START HERE

THE BASICS

I V vi IV

I IV V

ii V I

I vi IV V

BEYOND BASICS

WRITING SONGS

Scan to **HEAR** the C major chord, and access the full library of scales and chords on flametreemusic.com

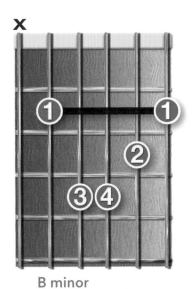

B minor

Chord Spelling

1st (B), ♭3rd (D), 5th (F♯)

E major

Chord Spelling

1st (E), 3rd (G♯), 5th (B)

A major

Chord Spelling

1st (A), 3rd (C♯), 5th (E)

FREE ACCESS on iPhone & Android etc, using any free QR code app

Scan to **HEAR** the C major chord, and access the full library of scales and chords on flametreemusic.com

START HERE

THE BASICS

I V vi IV

I IV V

ii V I

I vi IV V

BEYOND BASICS

WRITING SONGS

START
HERE

THE
BASICS

I V vi IV

I IV V

ii V I

I vi IV V

BEYOND
BASICS

WRITING
SONGS

ii V I Examples

This progression is extremely popular in jazz standards, though can also turn up on its own or as a bridging progression in other music styles. Often the basic **ii V I** is embellished and extended to create a range of different sounds. Below is a selection of songs that use this progression in some form.

Tune Up – Miles Davis
Satin Doll – Duke Ellington
Sunday Morning – Maroon 5
Pent-Up House – Sonny Rollins
Perdido – Juan Tizol
Still Got the Blues – Gary Moore
Spain – Chick Corea
It Don't Mean a Thing – Duke Ellington
Autumn Leaves (Jazz Standard)
All the Things You Are – Ella Fitzgerald
Honeysuckle Rose – Fats Waller
Stella by Starlight – Miles Davis
Giant Steps – John Coltrane
Blue Bossa – Kenny Dorham
Layla – Eric Clapton

Opposite are three examples of the **ii V I** sequence in action.

The first uses arpeggios for the progression in **D major.** The second example in **G major** follows its **ii V7 I** progression with chords IV and I.

The final example uses the progression in **A minor**, as **ii°7 V7 i.**

Scan to **HEAR** the C major chord, and access the full library of scales and chords on flametreemusic.com

Song 1

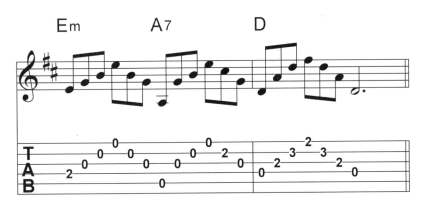

Song 2

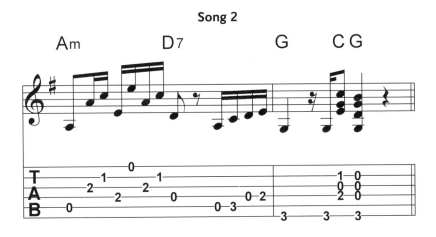

Song 3

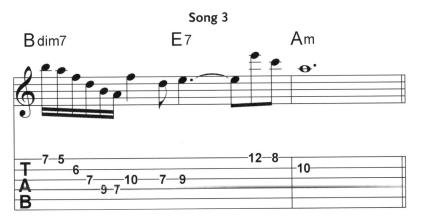

START
HERE

THE
BASICS

I V vi IV

I IV V

ii V I

I vi IV V

BEYOND
BASICS

WRITING
SONGS

FREE ACCESS on iPhone & Android etc, using any free QR code app

Scan to **HEAR** the C major chord, and access the full library of scales and chords on flametreemusic.com

Quick Reference

Here's an at-a-glance list of the **ii V I** progression in the most common keys, as covered in the previous pages.

START
HERE

THE
BASICS

I V vi IV

I IV V

ii V I

I vi IV V

BEYOND
BASICS

WRITING
SONGS

C Major

Dm	G	C
ii	V	I
minor 2nd	5th	1st

D Major

Em	A	D
ii	V	I
minor 2nd	5th	1st

E Major

F#m	B	E
ii	V	I
minor 2nd	5th	1st

G Major

Am	D	G
ii	V	I
minor 2nd	5th	1st

A Major

Bm	E	A
ii	V	I
minor 2nd	5th	1st

FREE ACCESS on iPhone & Android
etc, using any free QR code app

Scan to **HEAR** the C major chord, and
access the full library of scales and
chords on flametreemusic.com

START
HERE

THE
BASICS

I V vi IV

I IV V

ii V I

I vi IV V

BEYOND
BASICS

WRITING
SONGS

FREE ACCESS on iPhone & Android etc, using any free QR code app

Scan to **HEAR** the C major chord, and access the full library of scales and chords on flametreemusic.com

START
HERE

THE
BASICS

I V vi IV

I IV V

ii V I

I vi IV V

BEYOND
BASICS

WRITING
SONGS

Variations

As with the other progressions in this book, there are many different ways to use the basic **ii V I** progression in a piece of music. A popular use of the progression would include 7th chords, like the version on this page. It's also possible to use the progression in a minor key, as shown on pages 94–95.

Adding 7ths: ii7 V7 Imaj7

This includes the three different types of 7th chords: dominant 7ths, major 7ths and minor 7ths. We already know the triads needed for **ii V I** in C major, so we just need to find the 'seventh' note for for Dm, G and C. A reminder of each of the relevant major scales:

D major:	D	E	F♯	G	A	B	C♯
G major:	G	A	B	C	D	E	F♯
C major:	C	D	E	F	G	A	B

The ii chord is a minor triad, so we know to lower the F♯ of the D major chord to F. The 7th is also minor, so that becomes C rather than C♯. The V7 uses a dominant 7th, as the triad is major but the 7th is minor. Imaj7 refers to a major triad with a major 7th. So making the relevant changes to produce the **ii7 V7 Imaj7** progression:

ii	=	Dm (D, F, A) with added ♭7
ii7	=	**Dm7 (D, F, A, C)**
V	=	G (G, B, D) with added ♭7
V7	=	**G7 (G, B, D, F)**
I	=	C (C, E, G) with added major 7th
Imaj7	=	**Cmaj7 (C, E, G, B)**

All notes in the resultant chords are in the key of C (no sharps or flats), so the entirety of this progression will sound 'in key'. For more diagrams of common types of 7th chords, see pages 119–121.

Dm7

Chord Spelling

1st (D), ♭3rd (F), 5th (A), ♭7th (C)

G7

Chord Spelling

1st (G), 3rd (B), 5th (D), ♭7th (F)

Cmaj7

Chord Spelling

1st (C), 3rd (E), 5th (G), 7th (B)

START HERE

THE BASICS

I V vi IV

I IV V

ii V I

I vi IV V

BEYOND BASICS

WRITING SONGS

START HERE
THE BASICS
I V vi IV
I IV V
ii V I
I vi IV V
BEYOND BASICS
WRITING SONGS

The Minor ii V I

This is a more complicated variation than the previous progressions in this book, as it involves a minor key. But the principle is the same: using a scale to work out which notes for which chord are needed.

We'll use the notes of the A minor scale, as this is the relative minor of C major and is the most popular minor key.

There are 3 types of minor scale, but here we use the harmonic minor:

A	B	C	D	E	F	G♯
i	ii^{o}	III+	iv	V	VI	vii^{o}

So the chords for this progression in A minor are:

B^{o}	E	Am
ii^{o}	V	i
B diminished	**E major**	**A minor**

The progression opposite is a common version of this basic chord sequence in a minor key. 7ths are often added to the ii^{o} and V chords, to give:

$B^{\varnothing}$:	B	D	F	A
and E7:	E	G♯	B	D

Half-diminished (ø) chords are sometimes notated as 'm7♭5', as they're made up of minor 3rd, lowered 5th and minor 7th intervals.

For more information on minor scales, and obtaining chord progressions from minor scales, see the Beyond Basics section of this book.

FREE ACCESS on iPhone & Android etc, using any free QR code app

Scan to **HEAR** the C major chord, and access the full library of scales and chords on flametreemusic.com

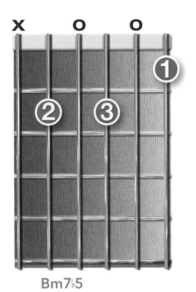

X   O   O   O

Bm7♭5

Chord Spelling

1st (B), ♭3rd (D), ♭5th (F), ♭7th (A)

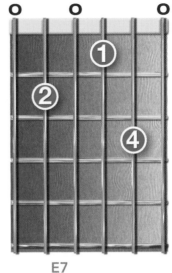

O   O   O

E7

Chord Spelling

1st (E), 3rd (G♯), 5th (B), ♭7th (D)

X   O   O

A minor

Chord Spelling

1st (A), ♭3rd (C), 5th (E)

START HERE

THE BASICS

I V vi IV

I IV V

ii V I

I vi IV V

BEYOND BASICS

WRITING SONGS

FREE ACCESS on iPhone & Android etc, using any free QR code app

Scan to **HEAR** the C major chord, and access the full library of scales and chords on flametreemusic.com

START
HERE

THE
BASICS

I V vi IV

I IV V

ii V I

I vi IV V

BEYOND
BASICS

WRITING
SONGS

I vi IV V

The final main chord progression focused on in this book is actually a variation of the first chord progression: I V vi IV. This is a different ordering of the same four chords that was immensely popular in the 20th century, and that is now often referred to as the '50s' chord progression.

Common variations include turning the final V chord into a V7, or substituting the vi chord for a ii chord. The following pages cover these variations, as well as giving the chord names and diagrams for the progression in **C major**, **D major**, **E major** and **A major**.

This section will cover:

- How I vi IV V relates to keys and scales
- I vi IV V shown in practice in the key of C
- I vi IV V transposed to other common keys: D, E, G and A
- Examples of I vi IV V in action
- Quick reference page of I vi IV V in the common keys
- Two variations of the progression to try out
- Clear chord names, chord diagrams and QR code links throughout

FREE ACCESS on iPhone & Android etc, using any free QR code app

Scan to **HEAR** the C major chord, and access the full library of scales and chords on flametreemusic.com

START
HERE

THE
BASICS

I V vi IV

I IV V

ii V I

I vi IV V

BEYOND
BASICS

WRITING
SONGS

FREE ACCESS on iPhone & Android etc, using any free QR code app

Scan to **HEAR** the C major chord, and access the full library of scales and chords on flametreemusic.com

START
HERE

THE
BASICS

I V vi IV

I IV V

ii V I

I vi IV V

BEYOND
BASICS

WRITING
SONGS

I vi IV V
in C

In C major, the chords needed for the **I vi IV V** progression are formed using the notes of the C major scale:

C	D	E	F	G	A	B
I	ii	iii	IV	V	vi	vii°

So the chords for this progression in C major are:

C	Am	F	G
I	vi	IV	V
C major	A minor	F major	G major

In a standard 4/4 song, with four beats per bar, these are the chords you would play:

C   /   /   /

Am   /   /   /

F   /   /   /

G   /   /   /

FREE ACCESS on iPhone & Android etc, using any free QR code app

Scan to **HEAR** the C major chord, and access the full library of scales and chords on flametreemusic.com

C major

Chord Spelling

1st (C), 3rd (E), 5th (G)

A minor

Chord Spelling

1st (A), ♭3rd (C), 5th (E)

F major

Chord Spelling

1st (F), 3rd (A), 5th (C)

G major

Chord Spelling

1st (G), 3rd (B), 5th (D)

START HERE

THE BASICS

I V vi IV

I IV V

ii V I

I vi IV V

BEYOND BASICS

WRITING SONGS

FREE ACCESS on iPhone & Android etc, using any free QR code app

Scan to **HEAR** the C major chord, and access the full library of scales and chords on flametreemusic.com

START
HERE

THE
BASICS

I V vi IV

I IV V

ii V I

I vi IV V

BEYOND
BASICS

WRITING
SONGS

Other Keys
I vi IV V in D

In D major, the chords needed for the **I vi IV V** progression are formed using the notes of the D major scale:

D	E	F♯	G	A	B	C♯
I	ii	iii	IV	V	vi	vii°

So the chords for this progression in D major are:

D	Bm	G	A
I	vi	IV	V
D major	B minor	G major	A major

In a standard 4/4 song, with four beats per bar, these are the chords you would play:

D / / /
Bm / / /
G / / /
A / / /

D major

Chord Spelling

1st (D), 3rd (F♯), 5th (A)

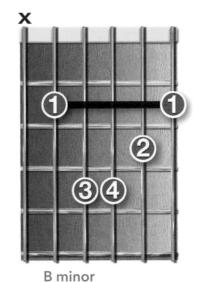

B minor

Chord Spelling

1st (B), ♭3rd (D), 5th (F♯)

G major

Chord Spelling

1st (G), 3rd (B), 5th (D)

A major

Chord Spelling

1st (A), 3rd (C♯), 5th (E)

START HERE

THE BASICS

I V vi IV

I IV V

ii V I

I vi IV V

BEYOND BASICS

WRITING SONGS

FREE ACCESS on iPhone & Android etc, using any free QR code app

Scan to **HEAR** the C major chord, and access the full library of scales and chords on flametreemusic.com

START
HERE

THE
BASICS

I V vi IV

I IV V

ii V I

I vi IV V

BEYOND
BASICS

WRITING
SONGS

Other Keys
I vi IV V in E

In E major, the chords needed for the **I vi IV V** progression are formed using the notes of the E major scale:

E	F♯	G♯	A	B	C♯	D♯
I	ii	iii	IV	V	vi	vii°

So the chords for this progression in E major are:

E	C♯m	A	B
I	vi	IV	V
E major	C♯ minor	A major	B major

In a standard 4/4 song, with four beats per bar, these are the chords you would play:

E / / /
C♯m / / /
A / / /
B / / /

Scan to **HEAR** the C major chord, and access the full library of scales and chords on flametreemusic.com

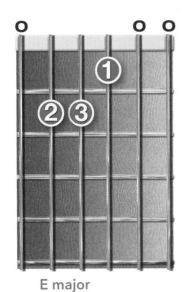

E major

Chord Spelling

1st (E), 3rd (G#), 5th (B)

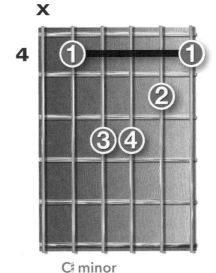

C# minor

Chord Spelling

1st (C#), b3rd (E), 5th (G#)

A major

Chord Spelling

1st (A), 3rd (C#), 5th (E)

B major

Chord Spelling

1st (B), 3rd (D#), 5th (F#)

Scan to **HEAR** the C major chord, and access the full library of scales and chords on flametreemusic.com

START HERE

THE BASICS

I V vi IV

I IV V

ii V I

I vi IV V

BEYOND BASICS

WRITING SONGS

START
HERE

THE
BASICS

I V vi IV

I IV V

ii V I

I vi IV V

BEYOND
BASICS

WRITING
SONGS

Other Keys
I vi IV V in G

In G major, the chords needed for the **I vi IV V** progression are formed using the notes of the G major scale:

G   A   B   C   D   E   F♯

I   ii   iii   IV   V   vi   vii°

So the chords for this progression in G major are:

G   Em   C   D

I   vi   IV   V

G major   E minor   C major   D major

In a standard 4/4 song, with four beats per bar, these are the chords you would play:

G / / /
Em / / /
C / / /
D / / /

FREE ACCESS on iPhone & Android etc, using any free QR code app

Scan to **HEAR** the C major chord, and access the full library of scales and chords on flametreemusic.com

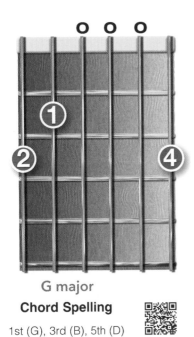

G major
Chord Spelling
1st (G), 3rd (B), 5th (D)

E minor
Chord Spelling
1st (E), ♭3rd (G), 5th (B)

C major
Chord Spelling
1st (C), 3rd (E), 5th (G)

D major
Chord Spelling
1st (D), 3rd (F♯), 5th (A)

START HERE

THE BASICS

I V vi IV

I IV V

ii V I

I vi IV V

BEYOND BASICS

WRITING SONGS

FREE ACCESS on iPhone & Android etc, using any free QR code app

Scan to **HEAR** the C major chord, and access the full library of scales and chords on flametreemusic.com

START
HERE

THE
BASICS

I V vi IV

I IV V

ii V I

I vi IV V

BEYOND
BASICS

WRITING
SONGS

Other Keys
I vi IV V in A

In A major, the chords needed for the **I vi IV V** progression are formed using the notes of the A major scale:

A	B	C♯	D	E	F♯	G♯
I	ii	iii	IV	V	vi	vii°

So the chords for this progression in A major are:

A	F♯m	D	E
I	vi	IV	V
A major	F♯ minor	D major	E major

In a standard 4/4 song, with four beats per bar, these are the chords you would play:

A / / /
F♯m / / /
D / / /
E / / /

A major

Chord Spelling

1st (A), 3rd (C♯), 5th (E)

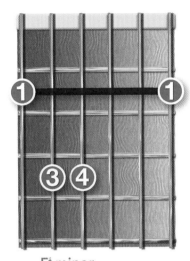

F♯ minor

Chord Spelling

1st (F♯), ♭3rd (A), 5th (C♯)

D major

Chord Spelling

1st (D), 3rd (F♯), 5th (A)

E major

Chord Spelling

1st (E), 3rd (G♯), 5th (B)

FREE ACCESS on iPhone & Android etc,
using any free QR code app

Scan to **HEAR** the C major chord, and
access the full library of scales and
chords on flametreemusic.com

Examples

As with the first progression covered in this book, the **I vi IV V** progression exists in much popular music due to the pleasing sound of those same four chords. Often, the V exists in its V7 form in order to lead the ear to the next chord. Below is a selection of tunes that use this progression in some form or other.

Stand by Me – Ben E. King
Blank Space – Taylor Swift
Wonderful World – Sam Cooke
Perfect – Ed Sheeran
I Will Always Love You – Whitney Houston
A Hard Day's Night – The Beatles
Every Breath You Take – The Police
Purple Rain – Prince
Let's Twist Again – Chubby Checker
The Reason – Hoobastank
Nothing's Gonna Stop Us Now – Starship
Uptown Girl – Billy Joel
YMCA – Village People
All I Want for Christmas Is You – Mariah Carey
Dance With Me Tonight – Olly Murs
Please Mr Postman – The Marvelettes
Crocodile Rock – Elton John and Bernie Taupin
Jesus of Suburbia – Green Day
Girl on Fire – Alicia Keys
Call Me Maybe – Carly Rae Jepsen

Opposite are two examples of the progression in use. The first sequence uses fifth chords in **A major**, beginning with a V chord before the **I vi IV V** is shown. The second example in **G major** uses an inversion of Gmaj7 to step down from the G (I) to Em (vi) in the bass.

FREE ACCESS on iPhone & Android etc, using any free QR code app

Scan to **HEAR** the C major chord, and access the full library of scales and chords on flametreemusic.com

START
HERE

THE
BASICS

I V vi IV

I IV V

ii V I

I vi IV V

BEYOND
BASICS

WRITING
SONGS

Song 1

Song 2

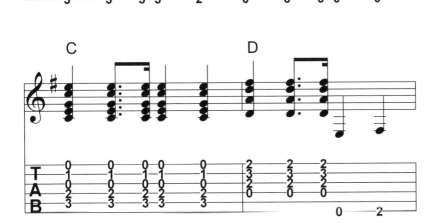

Scan to **HEAR** the C major chord, and access the full library of scales and chords on flametreemusic.com

START HERE

THE BASICS

I V vi IV

I IV V

ii V I

I vi IV V

BEYOND BASICS

WRITING SONGS

START
HERE

THE
BASICS

I V vi IV

I IV V

ii V I

I vi IV V

BEYOND
BASICS

WRITING
SONGS

Quick Reference

Here's an at-a-glance list of the I vi IV V progression in the most common keys, as covered in the previous pages.

C Major

C	Am	F	G
I	vi	IV	V
1st	6th minor	4th	5th

D Major

D	Bm	G	A
I	vi	IV	V
1st	6th minor	4th	5th

E Major

E	C#m	A	B
I	vi	IV	V
1st	6th minor	4th	5th

G Major

G	Em	C	D
I	vi	IV	V
1st	6th minor	4th	5th

A Major

A	F#m	D	E
I	vi	IV	V
1st	6th minor	4th	5th

FREE ACCESS on iPhone & Android etc, using any free QR code app

Scan to **HEAR** the C major chord, and access the full library of scales and chords on flametreemusic.com

START
HERE

THE
BASICS

I V vi IV

I IV V

ii V I

I vi IV V

BEYOND
BASICS

WRITING
SONGS

FREE ACCESS on iPhone & Android etc,
using any free QR code app

Scan to **HEAR** the C major chord, and
access the full library of scales and
chords on flametreemusic.com

Variations

The addition of a 7th or substitution of a chord are both common variations of the basic **I vi IV V** progression. Again, these progression variations are shown in C major but can easily be transposed to other keys using the roman numerals.

I vi IV V7

The most popular form of the **I vi IV V** progression is with a V7 chord. This is a simple but effective variation of the basic progression.

To recap, the V7 refers to a dominant 7th chord: the initial V triad is major, and the 7th is minor.

In C major, the chord V is G. To find the relevant 7th note to add to that V chord, we can therefore look at the scale of G major too:

C major:	C	D	E	F	G	A	B
G major:	G	A	B	C	D	E	F♯
	I	ii	iii	IV	V	vi	vii°

The V7 chord requires major 3rd and minor 7th intervals. So the B remains the same but the F♯ is lowered to an F, giving a complete chord of: G, B, D and F.

V7 chords are extremely popular as all the notes are part of the tonic key: all the notes of G7 are in the key of C major.

FREE ACCESS on iPhone & Android etc, using any free QR code app

Scan to **HEAR** the C major chord, and access the full library of scales and chords on flametreemusic.com

Sidebar navigation:
START HERE
THE BASICS
I V vi IV
I IV V
ii V I
I vi IV V
BEYOND BASICS
WRITING SONGS

START
HERE

THE
BASICS

I V vi IV

I IV V

ii V I

I vi IV V

BEYOND
BASICS

WRITING
SONGS

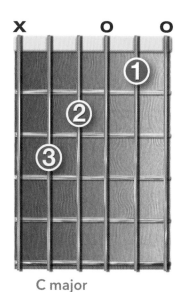

C major

Chord Spelling

1st (C), 3rd (E), 5th (G)

A minor

Chord Spelling

1st (A), ♭3rd (C), 5th (E)

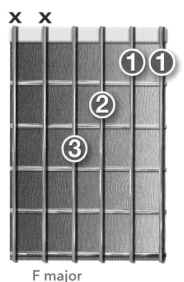

F major

Chord Spelling

1st (F), 3rd (A), 5th (C)

G7

Chord Spelling

1st (G), 3rd (B), 5th (D), ♭7th (F)

FREE ACCESS on iPhone & Android etc,
using any free QR code app

Scan to **HEAR** the C major chord, and
access the full library of scales and
chords on flametreemusic.com

START
HERE

THE
BASICS

I V vi IV

I IV V

ii V I

I vi IV V

BEYOND
BASICS

WRITING
SONGS

I vi ii V

Another common variation of the **I vi IV V** progression is to substitute a ii chord in place of the IV chord. Again, we've given it here only in C major, but it can easily be transposed to other keys using the techniques described previously.

As with the other progressions in this book, the chords needed for the **I vi ii V** progression in C major are formed using the notes of the C major scale:

C D E F G A B

I ii iii IV V vi vii°

So the chords for this progression in C major are:

C Am Dm G

I vi ii V

C major   A minor   D minor   G major

As has been seen with the first main progression in this book, the **I V vi IV**, it's possible to use the same four chords in a different order to create a new progression. This could apply here too, so play around with some inversions of the progression to get a feel for the different effects.

FREE ACCESS on iPhone & Android etc, using any free QR code app

Scan to **HEAR** the C major chord, and access the full library of scales and chords on flametreemusic.com

C major

Chord Spelling

1st (C), 3rd (E), 5th (G)

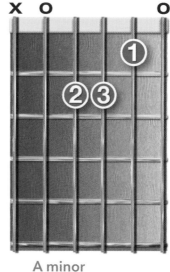

A minor

Chord Spelling

1st (A), ♭3rd (C), 5th (E)

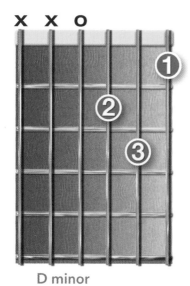

D minor

Chord Spelling

1st (D), ♭3rd (F), 5th (A)

G major

Chord Spelling

1st (G), 3rd (B), 5th (D)

START HERE

THE BASICS

I V vi IV

I IV V

ii V I

I vi IV V

BEYOND BASICS

WRITING SONGS

FREE ACCESS on iPhone & Android etc, using any free QR code app

Scan to **HEAR** the C major chord, and access the full library of scales and chords on flametreemusic.com

Advanced Techniques

Once you've got to grips with basic major and minor chords, all other chords can be understood as variations or extensions of those chords.

To convert the basic triads into other chords, all that's normally required is to add a note from the scale. You can also make your own interpretations of chords by using chord inversions, embellishments and substitutions instead of the original chords. This chapter introduces the many different ways to alter or decorate a chord progression.

This section will cover:

- Ways to embellish a chord progression
- Extended and altered chords: 7ths, 9ths, 11ths, 13ths, sus chords, 5th and 6th chords
- Inversions of progressions and the chords within them
- Adding more structure with moving bass lines
- Building progressions from minor scales
- Other chord progressions to try
- Other keys for reference

START HERE

THE BASICS

I V vi IV

I IV V

ii V I

I vi IV V

BEYOND BASICS

WRITING SONGS

START HERE

THE BASICS

I V vi IV

I IV V

ii V I

I vi IV V

BEYOND BASICS

WRITING SONGS

FREE ACCESS on iPhone & Android etc, using any free QR code app

Scan to **HEAR** the C major chord, and access the full library of scales and chords on flametreemusic.com

START
HERE

THE
BASICS

I V vi IV

I IV V

ii V I

I vi IV V

BEYOND
BASICS

WRITING
SONGS

Types of Embellishment

Chord embellishments are often easier to play than the basic major or minor chords. They vary the chord often by either substituting a note within it for a new note, or by adding an extra note. Whichever method is used, the new note is usually taken from the 'key scale' of the chord.

For example, you could add any note from the C major scale to the C major chord without changing the fundamental harmonic nature of the chord. By sticking to notes from the key scale, the new embellished chord can normally be used as a direct replacement for the simpler basic chord without causing any clashes with the melody of the song.

One of the most commonly used chord embellishments is the addition of a 7th note. There are three main types of 7th chords:

major seventh (maj7)

dominant seventh (7)

minor seventh (m7)

Only the major 7th chord uses the seventh note of the major scale; the other two types use the flattened seventh note of the scale.

FREE ACCESS on iPhone & Android
etc, using any free QR code app

Scan to **HEAR** the C major chord, and access the full library of scales and chords on flametreemusic.com

7th Chords

The dominant 7th chord is formed by taking the basic major chord and adding the flattened seventh note of the major scale to it. For example, C7 contains the notes: C, E, G, B♭.

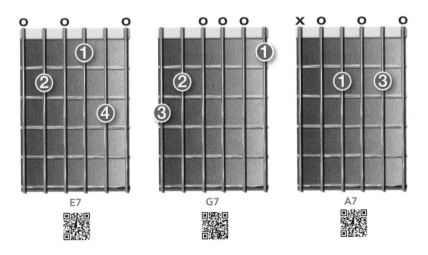

See **flametreemusic.com** for more Dominant 7th chords.

Scan to **HEAR** the C major chord, and access the full library of scales and chords on flametreemusic.com

START HERE

THE BASICS

I V vi IV

I IV V

ii V I

I vi IV V

BEYOND BASICS

WRITING SONGS

Major 7th Chords

The major 7th chord is formed by taking the basic major chord and adding the seventh note of the major scale to it. For example, Cmaj7 contains the notes: C, E, G, B.

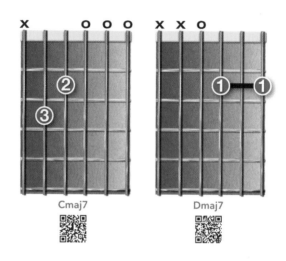

Cmaj7

Dmaj7

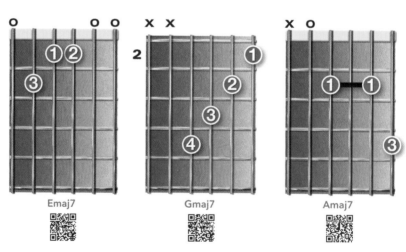

Emaj7

Gmaj7

Amaj7

See **flametreemusic.com** for more Major 7th chords.

Scan to **HEAR** the C major chord, and access the full library of scales and chords on flametreemusic.com

START HERE

THE BASICS

I V vi IV

I IV V

ii V I

I vi IV V

BEYOND BASICS

WRITING SONGS

Minor 7th Chords

The minor 7th chord is formed by taking the basic minor chord and adding the flattened seventh note of the major scale to it. For example, Cm7 contains the notes: C, E♭, G, B♭.

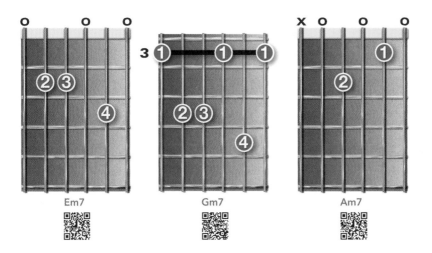

See **flametreemusic.com** for more Minor 7th chords.

FREE ACCESS on iPhone & Android etc, using any free QR code app

Scan to **HEAR** the C major chord, and access the full library of scales and chords on flametreemusic.com

START HERE

THE BASICS

I V vi IV

I IV V

ii V I

I vi IV V

BEYOND BASICS

WRITING SONGS

START
HERE

THE
BASICS

I V vi IV

I IV V

ii V I

I vi IV V

BEYOND
BASICS

WRITING
SONGS

Extensions

Using extended chords, containing five or six notes, helps to create a rich sound and to extend your chordal vocabulary. Altered chords provide an ideal method of creating a sense of tension and adding **harmonic dissonance** to a chord progression.

Just as 7th chords are built by adding an extra note to a basic triad, extended chords are built by adding one or more extra notes to a 7th chord. The most common types of extended chords are **9ths, 11ths and 13ths**. Each can be played in either a major, minor or dominant form.

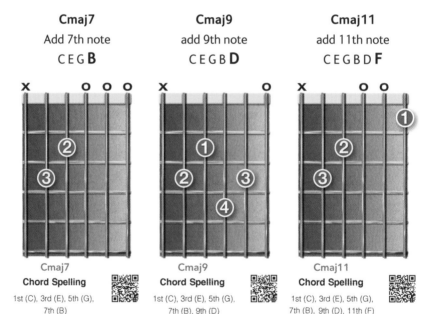

Cmaj7	Cmaj9	Cmaj11
Add 7th note	add 9th note	add 11th note
C E G **B**	C E G B **D**	C E G B D **F**

Cmaj7
Chord Spelling
1st (C), 3rd (E), 5th (G), 7th (B)

Cmaj9
Chord Spelling
1st (C), 3rd (E), 5th (G), 7th (B), 9th (D)

Cmaj11
Chord Spelling
1st (C), 3rd (E), 5th (G), 7th (B), 9th (D), 11th (F)

FREE ACCESS on iPhone & Android etc, using any free QR code app

Scan to **HEAR** the C major chord, and access the full library of scales and chords on flametreemusic.com

START
HERE

THE
BASICS

I V vi IV

I IV V

ii V I

I vi IV V

BEYOND
BASICS

WRITING
SONGS

There are quite a few commonly used chord embellishments that do not cause problems within an existing chord progression, as the basic chord's harmonic nature does not change.

Chord	Possible Embellishments
Major	major 6th, major 7th, major 9th, add9, sus2, sus4, major 6th add9
Minor	minor 7th, minor 9th, sus2, sus4
Dominant 7th	dominant 9th, dominant 13th, dominant 7th sus4

Raising or lowering the fifth and ninth intervals in chords can also create more colour within a piece. Jazz tunes in particular are based around extended chords (7ths, 9ths, 11ths and 13ths) and their alterations, so it helps to familiarize yourself with these in their various positions around the fingerboard. They are looked at in more detail over the following pages.

Scan to **HEAR** the C major chord, and access the full library of scales and chords on flametreemusic.com

START
HERE

THE
BASICS

I V vi IV

I IV V

ii V I

I vi IV V

BEYOND
BASICS

WRITING
SONGS

Cmaj9

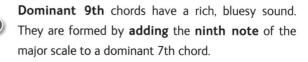

C9

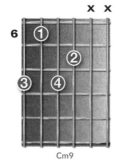

Cm9

Cadd9

9th Chords

Major 9th chords have a delicate sound that makes them highly suitable for use in ballads. They are extensions of major 7th chords, and are formed by adding the ninth note of the major scale (with the same starting note).

For example, **Cmaj9** contains the notes of **Cmaj7**: C E G B; plus the **ninth** note of the C major scale: **D**.

so **Cmaj9** is **C E G B D**

Dominant 9th chords have a rich, bluesy sound. They are formed by **adding** the **ninth note** of the major scale to a dominant 7th chord.

so **C Dominant 9th is C E G B♭** (the notes of C7) and **D** (9th note of C major scale)

Minor 9th chords have a suave, mellow sound and are often used in soul and funk music. They are extensions of minor seventh chords, formed by adding the ninth note of the major scale.

so **Cm9** is **C E♭ G B♭** (the notes of Cm7) and **D** (ninth note of the C major scale)

The ninth note can also be added to a simple triad, as this creates a certain warmth when added to a basic major chord.

So, add the ninth note D to the basic C major chord to become **Cadd9** (addition of ninth note D)

FREE ACCESS on iPhone & Android etc, using any free QR code app

Scan to **HEAR** the C major chord, and access the full library of scales and chords on flametreemusic.com

11th Chords

There are three main types of 11th chord. Each incorporates some form of ninth chord, plus the 11th note of the major scale.

Cmaj11

Cmaj11   C11   Cm11

Cmaj11 is **C E G B D F**

C11 is **C E G B♭ D F**

Cm11 is **C E♭ G B♭ D F**

C11

In practice, the ninth note is normally omitted when playing 11th chords on the guitar.

13th Chords

There are three main types of 13th chord.

Cm11

In practice, it is not possible to play all seven notes of a 13th chord on a guitar, therefore some notes (normally the 9th, 11th and sometimes the 5th) are omitted.

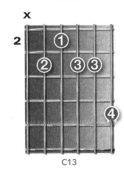

C13

so **C13** is **C E G B♭ D F A**

Scan to **HEAR** the C major chord, and access the full library of scales and chords on flametreemusic.com

START HERE

THE BASICS

I V vi IV

I IV V

ii V I

I vi IV V

BEYOND BASICS

WRITING SONGS

Sus chords

Some chords are formed by replacing a note, rather than adding one. In 'sus' chords, for example, the chord's third is replaced by the **fourth** note of the major scale in sus4 chords, and by the **second** note of the scale in sus2 chords.

If you lift the finger of the first string when playing an **open position D major** chord shape, it will become a Dsus2 chord.

D major
Chord Spelling
1st (D), 3rd (F♯), 5th (A)

Dsus2
Chord Spelling
1st (D), 2nd (E), 5th (A)

Some other useful sus chords below:

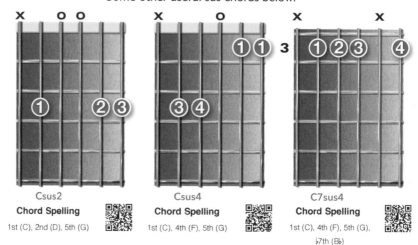

Csus2
Chord Spelling
1st (C), 2nd (D), 5th (G)

Csus4
Chord Spelling
1st (C), 4th (F), 5th (G)

C7sus4
Chord Spelling
1st (C), 4th (F), 5th (G), ♭7th (B♭)

Scan to **HEAR** the C major chord, and access the full library of scales and chords on flametreemusic.com

Power Chords

x   x x

3 ①

   ③④

C5
Chord Spelling
1st (C), 5th (G)

Power chords unusually do not include a major or minor third; they consist only of the root note and the fifth. They are common in rock music, where the root note and the fifth above it are played on the sixth and fifth, or fifth and fourth strings. With the right combination of electric guitar, amp and effects, this powerful sound characterizes hard rock and heavy metal.

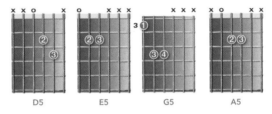

D5   E5   G5   A5

6th Chords

The sixth note of the major scale. For example, to play **C6** (C major 6th) you would play **C**, **E**, **G** and the sixth note of the major scale: **A**. Minor sixth chords are formed in the same way, by adding the sixth note of the major scale to the minor triad. So **Cm6** would be: **C, E♭, G, A**.

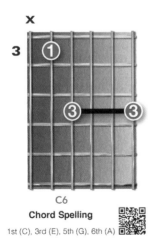

C6
Chord Spelling
1st (C), 3rd (E), 5th (G), 6th (A)

Cm6
Chord Spelling
1st (C), ♭3rd (E♭), 5th (G), 6th (A)

FREE ACCESS on iPhone & Android etc, using any free QR code app

Scan to **HEAR** the C major chord, and access the full library of scales and chords on flametreemusic.com

START HERE

THE BASICS

I V vi IV

I IV V

ii V I

I vi IV V

BEYOND BASICS

WRITING SONGS

START
HERE

Altered Chords

These are chords in which the fifth and ninth has been 'altered' – i.e. either raised or lowered by a half step. Altered chords are most commonly used in jazz.

THE
BASICS

Some examples of commonly used altered chords, and a reminder of their relevant symbols:

I V vi IV

Augmented triad:	+
Diminished triad:	°
Diminished 7th:	°7
Dominant 7th♭5:	7♭5
Dominant 7th♭9:	7♭9
Dominant 7th♯9:	7♯9

I IV V

ii V I

An augmented note refers to a **raised semitone**: in an augmented triad, the fifth has been sharpened.

I vi IV V

Diminished notes refer to **lowered semitones**: a diminished triad is made up of minor thirds.

BEYOND
BASICS

The chord diagrams for these altered chords in the key of C are shown on the opposite page.

WRITING
SONGS

FREE ACCESS on iPhone & Android etc, using any free QR code app

Scan to **HEAR** the C major chord, and access the full library of scales and chords on flametreemusic.com

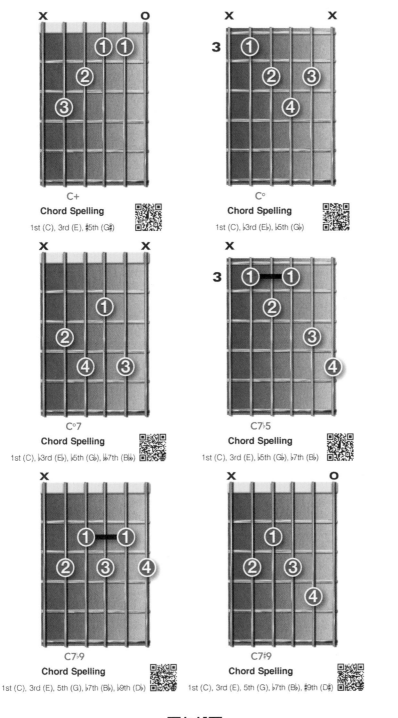

C+

Chord Spelling

1st (C), 3rd (E), #5th (G#)

C°

Chord Spelling

1st (C), ♭3rd (E♭), ♭5th (G♭)

C°7

Chord Spelling

1st (C), ♭3rd (E♭), ♭5th (G♭), ♭♭7th (B♭♭)

C7♭5

Chord Spelling

1st (C), 3rd (E), ♭5th (G♭), ♭7th (B♭)

C7♭9

Chord Spelling

1st (C), 3rd (E), 5th (G), ♭7th (B♭), ♭9th (D♭)

C7#9

Chord Spelling

1st (C), 3rd (E), 5th (G), ♭7th (B♭), #9th (D#)

Scan to **HEAR** the C major chord, and access the full library of scales and chords on flametreemusic.com

START HERE

THE BASICS

I V vi IV

I IV V

ii V I

I vi IV V

BEYOND BASICS

WRITING SONGS

Chord Inversions

Rather than play every chord starting from its root note, you can play an 'inversion' by choosing another chord tone as the lowest note. There are three main types of inversion:

First Inversion: 3rd of the chord is the lowest note

Second Inversion: 5th of the chord is the lowest note

Third Inversion: extension of the chord is the lowest note

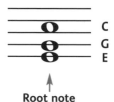

C Major 1st Inversion

3rd and 5th and octave notes of the C Major scale

C
G
E

Root note

Inversions are normally notated as 'slash chords': C/E is 'C major first inversion'

C/E	C/G	Cmaj7/B
(lowest note is E)	(lowest note is G)	(lowest note is B)

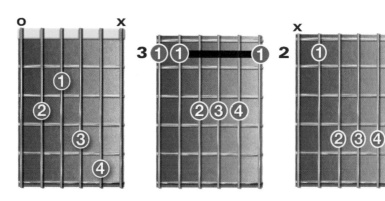

Scan to **HEAR** the C major chord, and access the full library of scales and chords on flametreemusic.com

Progression Inversions

It's also possible to invert the chord positions within an inversion. This could result in some of the variations we've seen already, such as the **I V vi IV** progression becoming **vi IV I V**, **I IV vi V**, or **I vi IV V**.

Chord Substitution

C major

A minor

An interesting effect can also be achieved by substituting one chord for another. For example, a major chord might be replaced by its **relative minor** (i.e. the minor chord with a root note three half steps lower). So **C major** might be **substituted** by **A minor**.

Alternatively, a minor chord could be replaced by its **relative major** (i.e. the major chord with a root note three half steps higher). So C major could be used in place of A minor.

Chord substitution is common in jazz – it's often done by taking a chord with a dominant seventh note, and replacing it with another chord with a root note a flattened fifth higher – for example, substituting a D♭7 chord for a G minor chord.

With chord substitution, the basic progression **C Am Dm G** could even become any of these progressions:

$$\| \text{Cmaj9} \mid \text{Am11} \mid \text{Dm9} \mid \text{G13} \|$$

$$\| \text{Cmaj9} \mid \text{Am7}\sharp 5 \mid \text{Dm7}\flat 5 \mid \text{G7}\sharp 5\sharp 9 \|$$

$$\| \text{Cmaj9} \mid \text{E}\flat 7 \mid \text{A}\flat 9 \mid \text{D}\flat 13 \|$$

START HERE

THE BASICS

I V vi IV

I IV V

ii V I

I vi IV V

BEYOND BASICS

WRITING SONGS

Adding More Structure

A way to add more structure to a chord progression is to make full use of the notes offered by the chords, by using a bass note that is not the root of the chord. This creates a moving line in the bass, giving a kind of melodic rhythm to the progression.

The next few pages look at these three types of moving bass lines:

- **Descending Bass Lines**
- **Ascending Bass Lines**
- **Alternating Bass Lines**

An alternating bass is when there is a return to the same bass note, usually every other chord, to deliver a strong sense of rhythm. Descending and Ascending bass lines move in regular steps in either direction, allowing a smooth transition between chords rather than hopping between notes in the bass. In the below example, the bass notes of the power chords descend in steps down to the G.

Slash chords – or inverted chords (see page 130) – can be used in order to create the bass line movement that you want to use.

FREE ACCESS on iPhone & Android etc, using any free QR code app

Scan to **HEAR** the C major chord, and access the full library of scales and chords on flametreemusic.com

START HERE

THE BASICS

I V vi IV

I IV V

ii V I

I vi IV V

BEYOND BASICS

WRITING SONGS

START
HERE

THE
BASICS

I V vi IV

I IV V

ii V I

I vi IV V

BEYOND
BASICS

WRITING
SONGS

FREE ACCESS on iPhone & Android etc, using any free QR code app

Scan to **HEAR** the C major chord, and access the full library of scales and chords on flametreemusic.com

Descending Bass Line

START
HERE

THE
BASICS

I V vi IV

I IV V

ii V I

I vi IV V

**BEYOND
BASICS**

WRITING
SONGS

Also known as a 'walkdown', or 'walking bass', a descending bass line moves down in steps. It is a popular way of linking chords together in a smooth and recognizable fashion.

A reminder of the C major scale:

C D E F G A B

I ii iii IV V vi viiº

A common descending bass in C would be to use a **Cmaj7/B** slash chord before an **Am** chord to connect the I and the vi of a progression smoothly. The notes in the bass line would therefore be **C, B** then **A**.

Look for chords that would contain the note you need, and rearrange the chord to fit the bass line you want.

For example, to carry the progression on further, you could next use a V chord in its root position or a I chord in its 2nd inversion, as that would give you a G.

To get an F in the bass you could use a IV chord in its root position, a ii chord in first inversion, or a V7 chord in 3rd inversion.

To achieve an E next in the bass you could use the I chord in its first inversion: **C/E** would give the notes **E, G** and **C**.

And so on. The chord diagrams opposite use the **C, Cmaj7/B, Am**, and **C/G** progression to demonstrate.

FREE ACCESS on iPhone & Android etc, using any free QR code app

Scan to **HEAR** the C major chord, and access the full library of scales and chords on flametreemusic.com

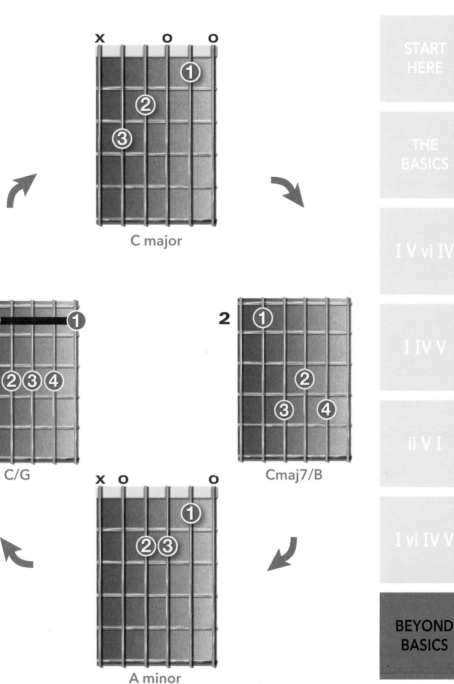

C major

C/G

Cmaj7/B

A minor

START HERE

THE BASICS

I V vi IV

I IV V

ii V I

I vi IV V

BEYOND BASICS

WRITING SONGS

FREE ACCESS on iPhone & Android etc, using any free QR code app

Scan to **HEAR** the C major chord, and access the full library of scales and chords on flametreemusic.com

Ascending Bass Line

This progression is similar to the descending bass line, but going in the opposite direction. An example would be the progression used in Bob Dylan's *Like a Rolling Stone*.

Again, we can use C major as an example. We're now familiar with the scale layout:

C	D	E	F	G	A	B
I	ii	iii	IV	V	vi	vii°

A relatively straightforward ascending bass line starting from C could be as follows:

Use the **I chord** in its root position: **C**

Then the **ii chord** in its root position: **Dm**

Then the **I chord** in its first inversion: **C/E**

Then the **IV chord** in its root position: **F**

This progression in C major is used to great effect in Led Zeppelin's *Fool in the Rain*.

The examples of ascending and descending bass lines in this book use steps of a tone, but it's also common to progress in **steps of other sizes**, like half-steps (semitones) or fourths or fifths. So if you begin on C, you could have an ascending bass in fourths that goes from C, to F, to B, to E.

FREE ACCESS on iPhone & Android etc, using any free QR code app

Scan to **HEAR** the C major chord, and access the full library of scales and chords on flametreemusic.com

START HERE

THE BASICS

I V vi IV

I IV V

ii V I

I vi IV V

BEYOND BASICS

WRITING SONGS

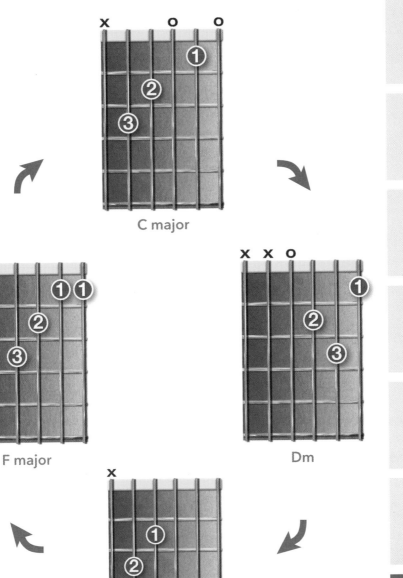

C major

F major

Dm

C/E

START
HERE

THE
BASICS

I V vi IV

I IV V

ii V I

I vi IV V

BEYOND
BASICS

WRITING
SONGS

FREE ACCESS on iPhone & Android etc, using any free QR code app

Scan to **HEAR** the C major chord, and access the full library of scales and chords on flametreemusic.com

Alternating Bass Line

Another way to add an interesting bass movement to your chord progressions is to use an alternating bass line. This involves the bass line moving back and forth between two notes.

If the picking pattern on a chord is repeated, then it's possible to use a different bass the second time. This will normally be another note from the chord, such as the 3rd or 5th, usually on the adjacent bass string. This technique can completely transform a simple chord progression, making it sound quite complex because of the moving bass line.

Here's the C major scale for reference again:

C   D   E   F   G   A   B
I   ii   iii   IV   V   vi   vii°

An example of an alternating bass in C major would be to use the C major chord in its root position, with the C as the bass, then use the same chord again but with the V (the G) as the bass note:

C   C/G   C   C/E

This could be played as a divided chord, with the bass note played first, and the rest of the chord following on the next beat.

Once the regularity of the return to the bass note has been established, the next chords in the series could move on to another chord from the scale, for example the G.

Scan to **HEAR** the C major chord, and access the full library of scales and chords on flametreemusic.com

START
HERE

THE
BASICS

I V vi IV

I IV V

ii V I

I vi IV V

BEYOND
BASICS

WRITING
SONGS

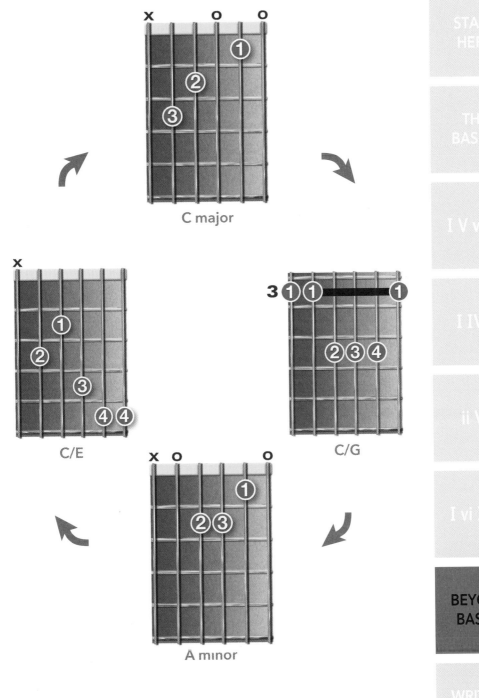

C major

C/E

C/G

A minor

START HERE

THE BASICS

I V vi IV

I IV V

ii V I

I vi IV V

BEYOND BASICS

WRITING SONGS

FREE ACCESS on iPhone & Android etc, using any free QR code app

Scan to **HEAR** the C major chord, and access the full library of scales and chords on flametreemusic.com

START
HERE

THE
BASICS

I V vi IV

I IV V

ii V I

I vi IV V

BEYOND
BASICS

WRITING
SONGS

Other Chord Progressions

Chord Progressions from Minor Scales

While there is only one major scale format, there are three types of minor scale:

- **The Natural Minor Scale**
- **The Harmonic Minor Scale**
- **The Melodic Minor Scale**

Progressions using minor scales will often borrow from other minor scales dependent on which notes they offer. The harmonic minor scale is useful, as the flattened 7th note allows a V7 chord to be formed. It differs from its major form with a flattened 3rd and a flattened 6th. So while the notes of A major would be:

$$ \text{A} \quad \text{B} \quad \text{C}\sharp \quad \text{D} \quad \text{E} \quad \text{F}\sharp \quad \text{G}\sharp $$

A minor harmonic would be:

$$ \text{A} \quad \text{B} \quad \text{C} \quad \text{D} \quad \text{E} \quad \text{F} \quad \text{G}\sharp $$

As the relative minor of C major, A minor is an easy one for us to start with. Its scale in standard and TAB notation would be:

FREE ACCESS on iPhone & Android etc, using any free QR code app

Scan to **HEAR** the C major chord, and access the full library of scales and chords on flametreemusic.com

A Minor Harmonic

A	B	C	D	E	F	G#
i	ii°	III	iv	V	VI	vii°
Am	B°	C+	Dm	E	F	G
Minor	Diminished	Augmented	Minor	Major	Major	Diminished

As with the major scales, the 1st, 3rd and 5th notes of the minor scale make up its minor triad. So the A minor triad contains the notes A, C and E. In C minor, this would be C, E♭ and G.

The harmonized scale gives us the chords that fit within this key:

i:	Am	(A, C, E)
ii°:	B°	(B, D, F)
III+:	C	(C, E, G#)
iv:	Dm	(D, F, A)
V:	E	(E, G#, B)
VI:	F	(F, A, C)
vii°:	G#°	(G#, B, D)

Other useful minor keys include: E minor, D minor and B minor, as these are relatively easy to play in, and so are more common.

Scan to **HEAR** the C major chord, and access the full library of scales and chords on flametreemusic.com

Sidebar navigation:
START HERE
THE BASICS
I V vi IV
I IV V
ii V I
I vi IV V
BEYOND BASICS
WRITING SONGS

The Minor i iv v

The chords needed for a **i iv v** progression in A minor can be formed using the A natural minor scale. This looks the same as C major (no sharps or flats), so doesn't have the G# that is present in the harmonic minor form. This in turn means that the v chord is minor: E, G, B.

A   B   C   D   E   F   G

i   ii°   III   iv   v   VI   VII

So the chords for this progression in A minor are:

Am   Dm   Em

i   iv   v

A minor   D minor   E minor

Using the scale to take the notes for each basic triad, we get:

A minor: A, C, E

D minor: D, F, A

E minor: E, G, B

See the chord diagrams opposite.

START HERE

THE BASICS

I V vi IV

I IV V

ii V I

I vi IV V

BEYOND BASICS

WRITING SONGS

A minor
Chord Spelling
1st (A), ♭3rd (C), 5th (E)

D minor
Chord Spelling
1st (D), ♭3rd (F), 5th (A)

E minor
Chord Spelling
1st (E), ♭3rd (G), 5th (B)

START
HERE

THE
BASICS

I V vi IV

I IV V

ii V I

I vi IV V

**BEYOND
BASICS**

WRITING
SONGS

FREE ACCESS on iPhone & Android etc, using any free QR code app

Scan to **HEAR** the C major chord, and access the full library of scales and chords on flametreemusic.com

START
HERE

THE
BASICS

I V vi IV

I IV V

ii V I

I vi IV V

BEYOND
BASICS

WRITING
SONGS

vi V IV III

Also known as the 'Andalusian Cadence', the **vi V IV III** progression is associated with a flamenco style, and offers a distinctive flavour. It can be heard in Del Shannon's 'Runaway'.

We can use the C major scale again to work out which chords to use:

C	D	E	F	G	A	B
I	ii	iii	IV	V	vi	vii°

So the chords for this progression in C major are:

Am	G	F	E
vi	V	IV	III
A minor	G major	F major	E major

As can be seen, this is a progression that descends in steps: the chord root notes go from A, to G, to F, to E. This doesn't quite translate from the major scale (where III is normally minor), as the G is sharpened to lead the ear back to the start of the progression.

The progression could also be understood in terms of a minor key.

Using a natural minor scale: i VII VI V
Using a harmonic scale: i ♭vii ♭vi V

Both these progressions, using A natural minor or A harmonic minor, would still produce the chords A minor, G major, F major and E major (again, the final chord being made major).

A minor
Chord Spelling
1st (A), ♭3rd (C), 5th (E)

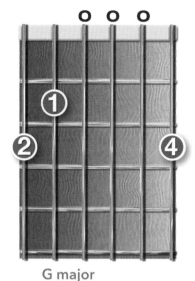

G major
Chord Spelling
1st (G), 3rd (B), 5th (D)

F major
Chord Spelling
1st (F), 3rd (A), 5th (C)

E major
Chord Spelling
1st (E), 3rd (G♯), 5th (B)

START HERE

THE BASICS

I V vi IV

I IV V

ii V I

I vi IV V

BEYOND BASICS

WRITING SONGS

FREE ACCESS on iPhone & Android etc, using any free QR code app

Scan to **HEAR** the C major chord, and access the full library of scales and chords on flametreemusic.com

START
HERE

THE
BASICS

I V vi IV

I IV V

ii V I

I vi IV V

BEYOND
BASICS

WRITING
SONGS

FREE ACCESS on iPhone & Android
etc, using any free QR code app

Scan to **HEAR** the C major chord, and
access the full library of scales and
chords on flametreemusic.com

Less Common Keys

There are **12 major keys** in western music. This book has focused on:

C major, D major, E major, G major, A major

These feature strongly in most of the popular music we hear around us. The other 7 major keys are:

B major, B♭ major C♯ major, E♭ major, F major, F♯ major A♭ major

Although you are unlikely to hear songs in those keys or want to write in them, it's useful to be aware of them for a fuller picture. Knowledge of them also provides a wider variety of chords for experimentation.

Each of the 12 keys also have their **minor** equivalents, which has been briefly introduced in the sections on **minor chord progressions**.

START HERE

THE BASICS

I V vi IV

I IV V

ii V I

I vi IV V

BEYOND BASICS

WRITING SONGS

FREE ACCESS on iPhone & Android etc, using any free QR code app

Scan to **HEAR** the C major chord, and access the full library of scales and chords on flametreemusic.com

START
HERE

THE
BASICS

I V vi IV

I IV V

ii V I

I vi IV V

BEYOND
BASICS

WRITING
SONGS

Writing Songs

It's one thing to be able to play through a given chord progression, but creating your own can be a different story. This chapter focuses on the songwriting aspect of playing chord progressions. It will show you how to make existing chord combinations more elaborate, as well as give tips on how to complement progressions with solo-playing.

Central to group composition too is the ability to communicate your ideas to others, so this chapter also offers a guide to typical chord charts.

This section will cover:

- **Basic song structures**
- **Styling your progression melodically and rhythmically**
- **Further techniques**
- **Playing in a group**
- **Chord charts and rhythm charts**
- **Progression movement in song structure: modulation and other combinations**
- **Soloing over progressions**

FREE ACCESS on iPhone & Android etc, using any free QR code app

Scan to **HEAR** the C major chord, and access the full library of scales and chords on flametreemusic.com

START HERE

THE BASICS

I V vi IV

I IV V

ii V I

I vi IV V

BEYOND BASICS

WRITING SONGS

FREE ACCESS on iPhone & Android etc, using any free QR code app

Scan to **HEAR** the C major chord, and access the full library of scales and chords on flametreemusic.com

Song Structure

There are no hard and fast rules when it comes to putting a song together, but having a clear basic structure **organizes** the song and gives obvious markers for the where the song is going, which is useful for a listener too.

It is worth listening to a wide range of material to get an idea of the formats available. Keep in the mind the style of song you want to produce, too.

Popular songs tend to work to a format, for example:

INTRODUCTION
VERSE
CHORUS
VERSE
CHORUS
MIDDLE EIGHT/INSTRUMENTAL BREAK
VERSE
CHORUS
CHORUS
END

This is a very typical format, and is known as an 'ABABCB' structure.

FREE ACCESS on iPhone & Android etc, using any free QR code app

Scan to **HEAR** the C major chord, and access the full library of scales and chords on flametreemusic.com

START HERE

THE BASICS

I V vi IV

I IV V

ii V I

I vi IV V

BEYOND BASICS

WRITING SONGS

- **THE INTRODUCTION is the exciting 'fingerprint' of the song that identifies and brings the first recognition of the song into view.**
- **The VERSE establishes the rhythm of the song, setting the scene for the chorus.**
- **The BRIDGE takes the song up a gear and lets you know that the chorus is coming.**
- **The CHORUS, when it comes, resolves all the tension that has been building up in the verse and bridge, and is usually the catchiest part.**
- **The MIDDLE EIGHT provides a little respite and sets the scene for the exciting introduction to appear again, while the final choruses and end section nail the point home.**

Not all songs include the bridge or 'middle 8' section, but generally the existence of that section in a song helps break up the repetitive structure.

Verses tend to be **quieter** than choruses and this contrast helps to add interest to the whole. The aim is to get a natural sense of light and shade between verse and chorus.

Much of rock rhythm playing will be **'straight eight'**, e.g. eight quavers to each bar. This gives the driving feel many rock songs need. The straight eight is generally played with down strokes only on the guitar's lowest strings, though variations may require a combination of up and down strokes.

START HERE

THE BASICS

I V vi IV

I IV V

ii V I

I vi IV V

BEYOND BASICS

WRITING SONGS

FREE ACCESS on iPhone & Android etc, using any free QR code app

Scan to **HEAR** the C major chord, and access the full library of scales and chords on flametreemusic.com

START
HERE

THE
BASICS

I V vi IV

I IV V

ii V I

I vi IV V

BEYOND
BASICS

WRITING
SONGS

Styling Your Progression

In standard chord charts, while the duration of each chord is clearly shown, the rhythm style that should be played is usually left to the discretion of the performer. This gives quite a bit of freedom in the playing of the chords.

- **Make sure your rhythm playing** relates to the musical style and mood of the song, but beyond that, you can experiment with a range of techniques to really make the progressions your own.

- **Remember that the chord progressions form the backbone of a piece of music**, so a repetitive, easily recognizable structure often identifies a song more than an eclectic mix of altered progressions. But the right bit of variety here and there can really spice up a progression and grip the listener in just the right way.

- From deciding **the number of strums per beat**, to **altering notes in the chords**, to **spreading the chord notes into arpeggio patterns**, there's a great deal that can be done to a basic chord progression.

The following pages cover the various melodic, rhythmic and technique-based decisions that can be made to create an arrangement that's truly unique.

FREE ACCESS on iPhone & Android etc, using any free QR code app

Scan to **HEAR** the C major chord, and access the full library of scales and chords on flametreemusic.com

START HERE

THE BASICS

I V vi IV

I IV V

ii V I

I vi IV V

BEYOND BASICS

WRITING SONGS

FREE ACCESS on iPhone & Android etc, using any free QR code app

Scan to **HEAR** the C major chord, and access the full library of scales and chords on flametreemusic.com

START
HERE

THE
BASICS

I V vi IV

I IV V

ii V I

I vi IV V

BEYOND
BASICS

More Ideas: Melodic Variety

There are many different ways of playing the same chord, so making a progression sound good is often just a case of **choosing the combinations** and chord formats that best suit your needs at the time.

You might want to **embellish** an existing chord, or add in a**nother chord**, or add in a few **different notes** here and there. It might be that you find **additional equipment** gives a stronger sound to your chords.

For example, humbucking pickups or valve amplification to 'fatten' the sound.

The following are just a few of the ways that you can add melodic variety to your progressions.

Developing Riffs

A riff is a short musical phrase that is repeated throughout a song, and is often what hooks a listener in. You may want to develop these riffs based on what's happening in the chordal accompaniment. This is likely to include a chord progression movement of some kind, even if all the chord notes aren't played.

Extended/Altered Chords

The use of extended or altered chords is a sure way to add variety to an otherwise basic chord arrangement. You can add other notes to create 7ths, 9ths, 11ths, or 13ths, or use sus and power chords to create particular sounds in the chord movement. Take a look back at pages 118-30 for a reminder of these techniques.

Passing Notes

You may want to use the scale you're in to include a few notes between chords. The **chromatic scale** (see page 172) is a useful scale to know if you'd like to include notes that aren't in the scale.

WRITING
SONGS

FREE ACCESS on iPhone & Android etc, using any free QR code app

Scan to **HEAR** the C major chord, and access the full library of scales and chords on flametreemusic.com

Added chords

Altering the combination of chords can change the function of a chord in a progression, but chords can also be added between your main chords to break up the patterns.

For example, sometimes chord changes are linked by chords a semitone higher or lower ('**approach chords**').

Some progressions also move forward by **returning to the same chord** every other chord.

A general example of this can be seen below, where the chord movement behind the melody notes in F minor is:

i7　iv7　i7　v7　i7

The return every other chord to the Fm7 chord strengthens the passage and fleshes out a basic minor **i　iv　v** progression.

START
HERE

THE
BASICS

I V vi IV

I IV V

ii V I

I vi IV V

BEYOND
BASICS

WRITING
SONGS

Timing

While that the rhythmic structure of chord progressions usually has to remain **recognizable and repetitive**, there are a number of timing techniques that can help give a **distinctive stylistic rhythm** to a piece. Incorporating rests or arpeggios into your chord progressions are a couple of easy features to try.

Note Lengths

Using chords of different lengths is one way to play with the timing of your progression. You can use a combination of **short and long notes**, while still keeping a regular rhythm. In the example below, the power chords are all played with the same rhythm, which would quickly become identifiable in a piece of music.

With distortion.

Syncopation, which shifts the emphasis of beats in a measure away from the obvious timing, is another useful technique to try out.

Rests

Rests between chords help add a well-defined rhythm to your progression, giving it musical shape and character.

Scan to **HEAR** the C major chord, and access the full library of scales and chords on flametreemusic.com

Arpeggios

An arpeggio is a **broken chord** in which the notes of the chord are played individually (rather than strummed simultaneously). As the notes of each arpeggio are taken from their chord equivalent, even when used soloing they can sound very tuneful and add colour to a chordal accompaniment.

C major arpeggio

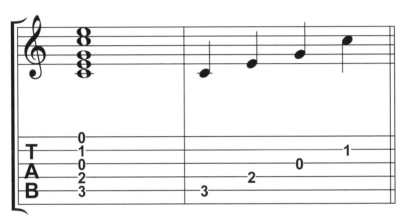

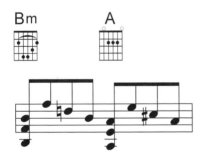

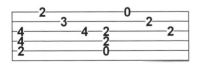

In this example, the notes for two chords in a progression are reinforced by descending arpeggios: B, D, F, and then A, C♯, E for the A chord.

START HERE

THE BASICS

I V vi IV

I IV V

ii V I

I vi IV V

BEYOND BASICS

WRITING SONGS

FREE ACCESS on iPhone & Android etc, using any free QR code app

Scan to **HEAR** the C major chord, and access the full library of scales and chords on flametreemusic.com

More Ideas: Technique

START
HERE

THE
BASICS

I V vi IV

I IV V

ii V I

I vi IV V

BEYOND
BASICS

WRITING
SONGS

Barre chords

Chords under solos may be played with open strings – most usually at the bottom end of the neck – or as barre chords, which can be **transposed** up the neck.

An alternative to open chords, the advantage of barre chords is that they allow the whole chord to be moved up the fingerboard to different pitches. This allows you to move **the same shape** up or down the fingerboard to create new chords without needing to memorize new fingerings each time. The trick is to choose the shape that will avoid any large fingerboard shifts.

Here is an **A minor barre chord** based on an **E minor** shape.

Moved down to the third fret, this becomes a **G minor chord**.

Moved up to the seventh fret, it becomes a **B minor chord**.

A minor
Chord Spelling
1st (A), ♭3rd (C), 5th (E)

Strum Patterns

Strumming chords is an essential technique to master, especially of course for rhythm guitar playing.

Make sure your standing or sitting position doesn't restrict the movement of your hands and arms, and keep a loose wrist action for the fingers to move freely.

Once you're familiar with the chord changes, try different combinations of down and upstrums. Omitting some bass strings on upstrokes and some treble strings on downstrokes will add variety.

You don't need to strum all the strings, particularly when playing upstrums. Try the top two strings, or bottom two strings, rather than the whole chord.

Fingerpicking

In some musical styles, more complex picking patterns might be used on the treble strings.

Once you are familiar with a pattern it's relatively easy to apply it to a chord progression. You just need to take care about which bass note to pick on each chord, ensuring you use the root note as your starting point.

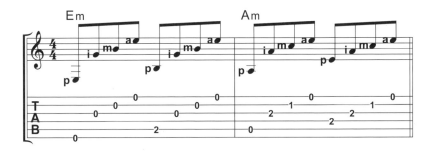

Scale Knowledge

Getting to know your scales will put you in an excellent position to dip in and out of keys where needed. Good scale knowledge will give you a strong idea of how each chord connects to another chord, and the directions the music can easily go.

Scan to **HEAR** the C major chord, and access the full library of scales and chords on flametreemusic.com

START HERE

THE BASICS

I V vi IV

I IV V

ii V I

I vi IV V

BEYOND BASICS

WRITING SONGS

START
HERE

THE
BASICS

I V vi IV

I IV V

ii V I

I vi IV V

BEYOND
BASICS

WRITING
SONGS

Playing Together

As a rhythm guitarist dealing with chord progressions, it is important when playing in a group to pay close attention to:

- **What the bass and drums are doing**
- **The first beat of each bar, which all elements should hit together**

The chord progression and riffs dictate what the lead guitarist will play, so a rhythm guitarist must lock into and augment the rhythm provided by bass and drums, acting as the link between that and the lead guitar and vocal.

Parts of the chord may be divided up between different instruments – e.g. the bass line might be dealt with or reinforced by another guitar – so communication is important.

FREE ACCESS on iPhone & Android etc, using any free QR code app

Scan to **HEAR** the C major chord, and access the full library of scales and chords on flametreemusic.com

Chord Charts

There are a few different ways to note down chord progressions. It's useful for **communicating** information to other players, and also good for your own memory recall, if you find yourself wanting to return to a progression you used in the past that you remember working well.

Simple chord charts are the most common way of notating the chord structure of a song or progression.

A chord chart normally has:

- **Each measure separated by a vertical line**
- **Two vertical lines indicating the end of the piece**
- **Chord symbols used to show which chords should be played**
- **The time signature written at the very beginning.**

If there is no time signature then it's usually safe to assume that the music is in 4/4 time.

When more than one chord appears in a single measure it can be assumed that the measure is to be evenly divided between the chords. In a song in 3/4 time, if three chords all appear in the same measure then you can assume that the measure is to be divided equally (one beat per chord).

Scan to **HEAR** the C major chord, and access the full library of scales and chords on flametreemusic.com

START HERE

THE BASICS

I V vi IV

I IV V

ii V I

I vi IV V

BEYOND BASICS

WRITING SONGS

START
HERE

THE
BASICS

I V vi IV

I IV V

ii V I

I vi IV V

BEYOND
BASICS

WRITING
SONGS

Chord charts are the most common method of notating the chord structure of a song or progression.

Using Chord Charts

Chord charts usually include a time signature, and in order to make the intention clear and avoid confusion, any division within a measure is shown by either a dot or a diagonal line after each chord: each dot or diagonal line indicates another beat. Below, each chord lasts for two beats.

In this kind of chord chart, while the duration of each chord is clearly shown, the rhythm style that should be played is left to the discretion of the performer.

Symbols

Chord charts are normally abbreviated by using 'repeat symbols' to indicate when the same chord is used again in the next measure.

𝄎   one bar is to be repeated exactly

·//·   more than one bar is to be repeated. The number of bars to be repeated is written above the symbol.

𝄆   the start of a section to be repeated

𝄇   the end of a section to be repeated. If repeated more than once, the number of times is written above this.

FREE ACCESS on iPhone & Android etc, using any free QR code app

Scan to **HEAR** the C major chord, and access the full library of scales and chords on flametreemusic.com

D.C.   (an abbreviation of Da Capo – play from the beginning)

D.S.   (an abbreviation of Dal Sego – play from the sign 𝄋)

Coda (refers to an end section, starting at the sign)

Fine   (end of the music)

If there are no dots at the start of the section, then repeat the music from the beginning of the piece. If two sections of music are identical, except for the last measure of measures, repeat dots are used along with first-time and second-time ending directions, like here:

‖: 4/4 Am | G | F

1. | Em :‖ 2. | Dm | Am ‖

Should be played as

‖ 4/4 Am | G | F | Em

| Am | G | F | Dm | Am ‖

Scan to **HEAR** the C major chord, and access the full library of scales and chords on flametreemusic.com

START HERE

THE BASICS

I V vi IV

I IV V

ii V I

I vi IV V

BEYOND BASICS

WRITING SONGS

Rhythm Charts

While standard chord charts are commonly used by pop and rock bands, a chord chart often does not give a clear idea about the rhythm to be used. More detailed and complex charts known as 'rhythm charts' are often presented to guitarists involved in recording sessions and those who play in theatre and function band settings. It helps to have familiarity with these.

A typical rhythm chart could be laid out like this:

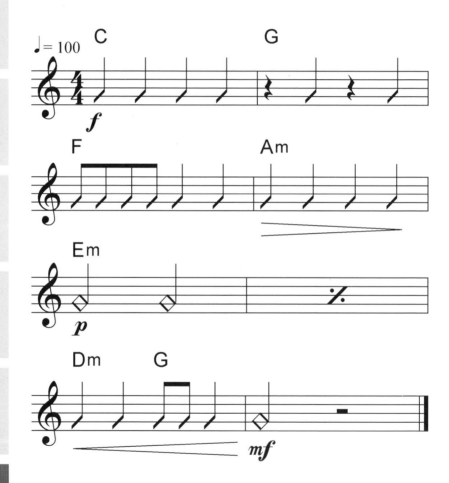

Scan to **HEAR** the C major chord, and access the full library of scales and chords on flametreemusic.com

START HERE · THE BASICS · I V vi IV · I IV V · ii V I · I vi IV V · BEYOND BASICS · WRITING SONGS

As a bridge between a chord chart and full-blown musical notation, rhythm notation consists of **pitchless notes and rests**. The type of note used tells you how many beats a chord lasts; the type of rest used tells you how many beats a silence lasts.

The note durations are the same as in regular music, so here's a quick reminder of the note and rest symbols and their relative lengths:

NAME	NOTE	REST	DURATION IN 4/4 TIME
Semibreve (whole note)	𝅝	▬	4 beats
Dotted Minim	𝅗𝅥.	▬·	3 beats
Minim (half note)	𝅗𝅥	▬	2 beats
Dotted Crotchet	♩.	𝄽.	1 ½ beats
Crotchet (quarter note)	♩	𝄽	1 beat
Dotted Quaver	♪.	𝄾.	¾ beat
Quaver (eighth note)	♪	𝄾	½ beat
Semiquaver (sixteenth note)	♬	𝄿	¼ beat

As with regular music, you may also come across **ties** (a curved line joining two notes of the same pitch) and **triplets** (where 3 notes should be played in the space of 2 notes of the same value).

Scan to **HEAR** the C major chord, and access the full library of scales and chords on flametreemusic.com

START
HERE

THE
BASICS

I V vi IV

I IV V

ii V I

I vi IV V

BEYOND
BASICS

**WRITING
SONGS**

Modulation

Movement to different keys can sometimes be heard, especially in Jazz music. The difference in key is marked by a distinct change in tonality, with confirmation of the new key often being reinforced using its primary chords in strong cadences.

If looking out for modulation in a piece of music, watch out for the type and frequency of **accidentals**.

If the same accidentals recurr it can suggest movement to a new key, for example to the **dominant** key (such as C major to G major) or **relative minor** (such as movement from C major to A minor).

It's common to use chords that are **shared** by both keys in order to make the transition smoothly.

START
HERE

THE
BASICS

I V vi IV

I IV V

ii V I

I vi IV V

BEYOND
BASICS

WRITING
SONGS

Scan to **HEAR** the C major chord, and access the full library of scales and chords on flametreemusic.com

Combining Progressions

While that it's important to retain the distinctive feel of a song, that is not to say that progressions cannot be combined. You may find that a repetitive progression throughout a song section can be broken up with a different progression to surprise the listener.

As well as substituting different chords into a progression, substituting **whole progressions** into a lengthier structure can have a similar effect. For example, you may want to try substituting a **ii V I** progression into a twelve-bar blues section, to introduce the added element of the ii chord.

As always, play around with **different combinations** and explore chord fingerings to suit your playing style. Knowledge of a wide range of chord types will enable you to play and adapt chord progressions for almost any musical genre, and will provide a platform for writing your own songs.

START
HERE

THE
BASICS

I V vi IV

I IV V

ii V I

I vi IV V

BEYOND
BASICS

WRITING
SONGS

FREE ACCESS on iPhone & Android etc, using any free QR code app

Scan to **HEAR** the C major chord, and access the full library of scales and chords on flametreemusic.com

Soloing over Progressions

The arena of lead-guitar playing requires knowledge of scales, or rather, a knowledge of patterns across the fretboard. Most solos start on the root note of the chord and progress up or down the scale, in various forms. Solos therefore work closely with the chordal accompaniment. Some notes feel 'right' and some don't, often because of their harmonic ties with what is going on in the chords.

Solos based on Major Pentatonic Scales

The pentatonic scale is a popular scale for improvising, as it has **fewer notes** than the standard 7-note scales, so there is less chance of any of the notes clashing with the accompanying chords. Here is the major pentatonic scale in C, though as we have seen with other scales, the basic structure can be applied to all keys.

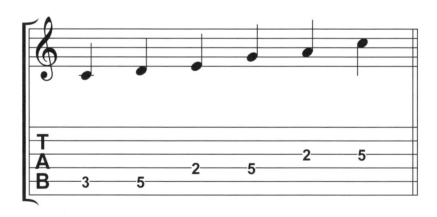

C Major Pentatonic • Notes: C, D, E, G, A, C
This scale works well over the chords C, Am, Gsus2 and Dsus2.

Scan to **HEAR** the C major chord, and access the full library of scales and chords on flametreemusic.com

The sidebar navigation tabs:
START HERE
THE BASICS
I V vi IV
I IV V
ii V I
I vi IV V
BEYOND BASICS
WRITING SONGS

START
HERE

THE
BASICS

I V vi IV

I IV V

ii V I

I vi IV V

BEYOND
BASICS

Minor Pentatonic Scales

Normally a minor scale can only really be played in a minor key and a major in a major key, but playing a pentatonic minor solo over a major chord progression results in flattened or 'blue' notes.

There are many different approaches to soloing over a progression, but the simplest way to learn is to target the **root notes** of each chord in the progression. If you were playing a blues song in the key of C, you may want to use the chords **C7, F7 and G7**.

To solo over those chords you could begin by playing the C pentatonic minor scale and targeting the notes C, F and G (which are all in the scale) over their respective chords.

Try bending or sliding to these notes to make things sound more bluesy.

C Minor Pentatonic • Notes: C, E♭, F, G, B♭, C

This scale works well over the chords Cm, C7, G7 and E♭.

FREE ACCESS on iPhone & Android etc, using any free QR code app

Scan to **HEAR** the C major chord, and access the full library of scales and chords on flametreemusic.com

Tips for Soloing

Using Scales

Scales are really suitable for **soloing** over a **chord sequence**. Once you've selected a scale to use, this will set the range of notes that will fit with the **backing chords**. When starting out, it can be helpful to **spell out** the chords to see which notes they have in common, before choosing relevant scales.

However, you don't need to play all the notes of the scale, or play them in any set order. You should always aim to make your solo sound **fresh and inventive**, rather than scale-like.

Phrasing

Once you've spent hours practising a scale it's all too easy to keep playing it in a continuous way when soloing. Here are some ways to break this habit:

- **Leave spaces between notes so that you start to create short phrases**
- **Use notes of different lengths within the phrases**
- **Vary the direction in which you play**

This rhythmic variety will add interest and shape to your phrases.

To start with, experiment with the C major scale; instead of playing it in strict time, leave some gaps, and balance some longer, **sustained** notes with some very quick **short** notes. There's also no need to play up the whole range of the scale before you play some descending notes – adopt a melodic approach in which your improvisation can **weave** up and down the scale.

START HERE

THE BASICS

I V vi IV

I IV V

ii V I

I vi IV V

BEYOND BASICS

WRITING SONGS

FREE ACCESS on iPhone & Android etc, using any free QR code app

Scan to **HEAR** the C major chord, and access the full library of scales and chords on flametreemusic.com

Using Intervals

One thing that always makes a solo sound too scale-like is using notes that are **adjacent** to each other in a scale. This type of playing gives the game away to the listener – they can hear, almost instantly, that the improvisation is derived from a scale. Using **interval gaps** when playing a scale is a perfect way to break away from this scalic sound.

Repetition

By repeating short series of notes you will begin to establish phrases that will give your solo a sense of **structure**. By repeating these phrases, or **variations** on them, you will give the listener something recognizable to latch on to, instead of a seemingly random series of notes with no direction.

Extra Techniques

String bends, vibrato, slides or slurs will all help give your solo an individual **character** and will turn it from a melody into a true guitar solo.

Listen carefully to what is being played on other instruments and your own, trying to make your solo **relate** to the overall musical style of the song.

Scan to **HEAR** the C major chord, and access the full library of scales and chords on flametreemusic.com

START HERE

THE BASICS

I V vi IV

I IV V

ii V I

I vi IV V

BEYOND BASICS

WRITING SONGS

START
HERE

THE
BASICS

I V vi IV

I IV V

ii V I

I vi IV V

BEYOND
BASICS

WRITING
SONGS

Other Useful Scales for Soloing

As well as the basic major and minor scales, there are a few other scales that could come in handy when constructing solos.

The Blues Scale

The Blues scale is often used over major chord progressions, and forms the basis of a lot of blues lead-guitar playing. It is well suited to **dominant seventh** chords.

Notes: C, E♭, F, G♭, G♮, B♭, C

This scale works well with the chords: C7, F7 and G7.

The Mixolydian Mode

When a major scale begins on on a different note, it produces a set of '**modes**'. For example, a major scale can be played on its second, or third, or fourth, or any other of its degrees, in order to produce a different set of interval structures and sounds.

When played on its fifth degree, it produces a Mixolydian modal scale. So if C major is played using G as its key note, that would give us the **G Mixolydian scale**.

FREE ACCESS on iPhone & Android etc, using any free QR code app

Scan to **HEAR** the C major chord, and access the full library of scales and chords on flametreemusic.com

Notes: G, A, B, C, D, E, F, G

This scale works well with the chords: G, G7, G9, C, Gsus2, G7sus4 and Dm.

When compared to the major scale with the same starting note (G major), the only difference is the flat 7 note (the B here). This gives the scale a bluesy yet melodic sound, which is why it is often used in blues, rock, jazz and folk music.

The Chromatic Scale

This scale does not relate to a particular key, as it contains every semitone (or half-step) between the starting note and its octave. Notes from the chromatic scale can be added to introduce notes that are not in the key of the chordal accompaniment. These 'outside' notes are known as **'chromatic' or 'passing' notes,** and help provide moments of harmonic tension.

FREE ACCESS on iPhone & Android etc, using any free QR code app

Scan to **HEAR** the C major chord, and access the full library of scales and chords on flametreemusic.com

START HERE

THE BASICS

I V vi IV

I IV V

ii V I

I vi IV V

BEYOND BASICS

WRITING SONGS

START
HERE

THE
BASICS

I V vi IV

I IV V

ii V I

I vi IV V

BEYOND
BASICS

WRITING
SONGS

Resources

Here are a few companion titles that could come in useful if you intend to develop your skills playing and songwriting for the Guitar.

Guitar Chords Card Pack

This pack of cards introduces common chord structures and encourages experimentation with the most popular chords, with one clear guitar diagram per card.

Guitar Chords

A handy reference, this book can sit beside you as you play. The most useful chords are arranged clearly per key, with one labelled chord per page.

Classic Riffs: Licks & Riffs in the Style of Great Guitar Heroes

Over 70 riffs feature in this collection of riff styles. Play like Ritchie Blackmore, Jimmy Page, Slash, Kurt Cobain and more, with riffs written in standard notation and tablature.

FREE ACCESS on iPhone & Android etc, using any free QR code app

Scan to **HEAR** the C major chord, and access the full library of scales and chords on flametreemusic.com

Scales for Great Solos

A guide to the most common scales in all the keys, clearly laid out with one scale per page with links to flametreemusic.com so you can hear how each scale sounds. Also includes tips on soloing, and the best scales to use for different chords and music styles.

How to Read Music: Essential Skills

The essentials for understanding music notation: pitch, clefs, rhythm, keys, scales and chords. Useful for both reading music and writing your own.

The Definitive Guitar Handbook

This 2017-updated comprehensive handbook follows through basic guitar skills to more complex techniques, as well as advice on stagecraft, performance and guitar maintenance. Includes a chord dictionary and galleries of guitars and guitarists.

All available at your local independent bookshop, instrument store, online, or direct from **flametreepublishing.com**

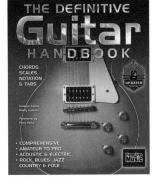

Also complementing this series is the audio library of chords and scales on flametreemusic.com, more details of which can be found on page 176.

FREE ACCESS on iPhone & Android etc, using any free QR code app

Scan to **HEAR** the C major chord, and access the full library of scales and chords on flametreemusic.com

START
HERE

THE
BASICS

I V vi IV

I IV V

ii V I

I vi IV V

BEYOND
BASICS

WRITING
SONGS

flametreemusic.com

The Flame Tree Music website complements our range of print books and offers easy access to chords and scales online, and on the move, through tablets, smartphones, and desktop computers.

1. The site offers access to chord diagrams and finger positions for both the guitar and the piano/keyboard, presenting a wide range of sound options to help develop good listening technique, and to assist you in identifying the chord and each note within it.

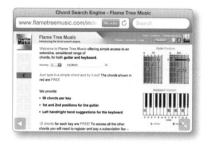

2. The site offers 12 **free** chords, those most commonly used in bands and songwriting.

3. A subscription is available if you'd like the full range of chords, **50** for **each key**.

4. Guitar chords are shown with **first** and **second positions on the fretboard**.

5. For the keyboard, you can **see** and **hear** each note in **left-** and **right-hand positions**.

6. Choose the key, then the chord name from the drop down menu. Note that the **red chords** are available **free**. Those in blue can be accessed with a subscription.

7. Once you've selected the chord, press **GO** and the details of the chord will be shown, with chord spellings, keyboard and guitar fingerings.

8. Sounds are provided in four easy-to-understand configurations.

9. flametreemusic.com also gives you access to **20 scales for each key**.